GEORGE TSYPIN OPERA FACTORY
Building in the Black Void

GEORGE TSYPIN

with texts by Julie Taymor and Grigory Revzin

Princeton Architectural Press, New York

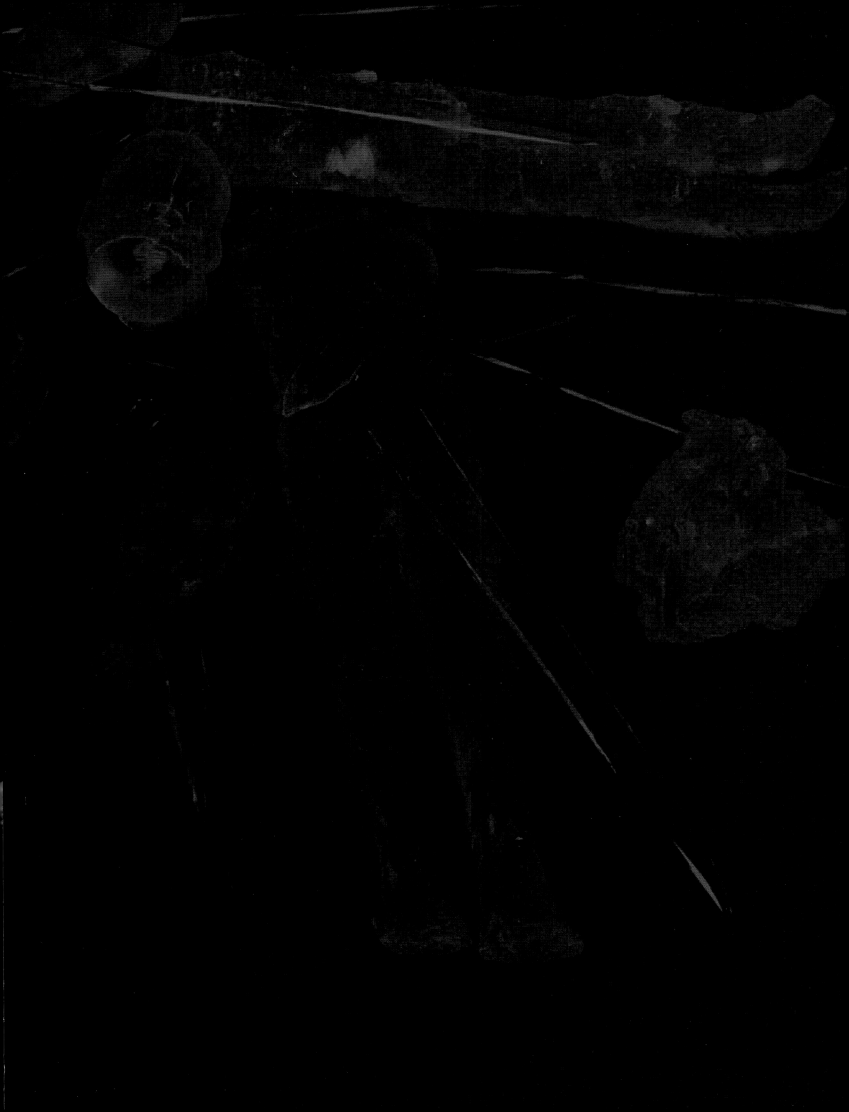

A huge city enveloped in dense gloom

Its streets the criss-crossed lines of children's notebooks.

It's here that the enormous madhouse looms.

A void within the order of the cosmos.

Joseph Brodsky

Table of Contents

Prelude

The Alchemy of Making an Opera ...15

Overture

Broken Myth ...19

Grigory Revzin

Acknowledgments

Theater is an effort in which it is very difficult to separate one person's work from the whole. A good production is always a fusion of energies, sometimes the most contradictory, of very different talents and personalities. I had the audacity to call the work in this book my own, but I know that it is the result of many collaborations. I can only mention a few here. I have been lucky: I have met the most incredible people in my life.

Peter Sellars has been the most important influence on my work. He goes places nobody else dares to go and achieves greatness on the way. Not only did he "discover" me right after I finished school, but he allowed me to discover myself. Julie Taymor is a unique talent, a demanding and brilliant collaborator. Francesca Zambello, always beaming with breathtaking artistic energy, is a true master of clarity and a friend. Joe Clark is a genius technical director, perhaps a superman. Pierre Audi is both an eccentric and elegant artist and an enormously powerful producer. Jürgen Flimm is a real man of theater and fun to be with. The film director Andrei Konchalovsky really expanded my horizons. Special thanks to Mimi Lien for her hard work in organizing materials for this book, to Allie Tsypin (my daughter) for steady moral and linguistic support, and to Clare Jacobson for giving it a shape. And of course Valery Gergiev has been an inspiration, a volcanic presence in my creative life for the last ten years.

Prelude

The Alchemy of Making an Opera

Lights beginning to dim, the audience finally takes its seats, conversation dies down, and finally…darkness. No matter when and where, or how many times you've seen the show, your heart stops in anxious anticipation. This is the most mysterious moment. In this black void the universe is about to be created, bursting out of the blackness…nothingness…negative space.

Daniel Barenboim once told me that he really conducts the silence between the notes. The moment of darkness before the show is the essence of theater as the performance itself becomes that pause in our lives, a moment of silence through music, a meditation about life, love, and death. It is a journey into the negative space as things that are normally obscured become transparent, a sort of X-ray of the soul…

Wagner's *Ring* starts in total blackness with one note: E Flat. Most musicians agree it is the tone of the earth. Then the tiny light of the conductor's baton appears, exploding into multitudes of stars and finally into a blinding beam of light. This is the creation of the world, the world that will disappear in the next instant. In opera, this most ephemeral and mortal medium, nothing can be fixed or repeated. Each moment is unique. Each gesture, sound, and image will dissolve into eternity. Opera is an attempt to build the City of Immortals with the most mortal building materials: music and light.

In 1913, Malevich along with his friends, poets Kruchenykh and Matushin, created a futurist opera, *Victory Over the Sun*. It's not an accident that while designing the sets for this opera, he created the most important work in his oeuvre, as well as the most seminal work in all of modern art. While he was working on one of the backdrops depicting an astronomical map in the form of dynamic movement and geometric shapes, suddenly he realized that all numbers, arrows, words, and anything reminiscent of this world had to be removed. In other words, it became an expression of the will of its creator and nothing else.

Soon after, the main event of his life took place. As the image of eclipse from the opera dominated his thoughts, he literally "eclipsed"—painted over his color geometric composition with black. This painting became known as *Black Square*, and was the foundation of suprematism. That was the image of nothing, the Black Void, a truly "Russian" darkness, a total Blackness of the soul, the universe without light—a stage.

My early training as an architect remains a main impulse in my work. In the Moscow Institute of Architecture, where I studied, some of the surviving members of the Russian avant-garde were still teaching. Sometimes, some of the most famous names in the West were reduced to mixing clay in the sculpture department. In the late seventies, I was one of the participants and winners of the competition, "New Spontaneous Ideas for the Theater of the Future," at the Centre George Pompidou in Paris. That was the beginning of the so-called Paper Architecture movement in Russia. The members of this group, many of them urban designers like me, created wildly imaginative projects, Utopian visions of the future that were intentionally unbuildable but rather served as social, philosophical commentaries and spiritual parables, kind of meta-stories told in space.

I started as an architect and urban planner of the most grandiose, Utopian schemes for whole cities, countries, for the Earth. I became a designer for opera, creator of the most intimate, personal, irrational visions. I travel around the world, I imagine the sets I design as fragments, ruins of some fantastic city, the Tower of Babel collapsing, shattering in front of my eyes. I see the memories, shadows of the sets I designed strewn across the landscape as I continue this futile attempt to rebuild this ideal, invisible, transparent nonexistent city that can only be found by traveling inside yourself: the City of Immortals.

I see my role as a designer for opera as equal to that of the composer, conductor, and director. But because of the scale of the space, the demands of today's visual culture, and the structural rigor of the musical score, the role of the artist sometimes transcends all others in making a plastic, emotional poem that creates a direct contact with the music. Sometimes it even goes against the music, but always creates a direct electrical charge between the sculptural space, color, light, and sound. The paradox of designing an opera is that while you have to use existing materials on this Earth (the only ones available), you aim at achieving an emotional impact and creating an atmosphere that is of another world. It's a search for the City of Immortals. A futile search. You work against yourself. You build the sets in order to destroy them. Through the alchemy of mixing metal, wood, glass, and stone, you are reaching for pure spirit, emptiness.

In string theory, the world is imagined as a symphonic whole made of tiny strings which are nothing but miniscule waves of energy, vibrating with different intensities. And there is nothing else. The entire matter, earth, atoms, neurons, gravitons, sun, galaxies, everything is made of these vibrational patterns, as if there is a tiny violin playing this very complex cosmic melody of the evolution of the universe. For symbolists a hundred years earlier, it was "the rhythm" or "incalculable, musical time . . . the musical wave effusing from the global orchestra." Meanwhile for Kandinsky, the "inner sound" undermined the cult of objects. In encountering the "new harmony," the object diffused and "vanished like smoke."

This book is about the alchemy of making an opera as the most synthetic form of spectacle from the point of view of the visual artist. While the musicians have the score, the artist has to start from scratch—every time. From the blackness of the Void, the universe is created. Creatively you go through four stages, four elements are needed: Water, Air, Earth, and Fire. As in Wagner's *Ring Cycle*, the book has four chapters: Water is the realm of the subconscious and of dreams, chaos, madness; Air is Space and the breadth of Imagination; Earth is Time and Memory; Fire is Light and Sun, a creative burn without a trace. It is the progression from black square (or rather black cube) through blue, gold, and red into blazing white light.

Overture

Broken Myth

Grigory Revzin

George Tsypin is a rare example of a contemporary Russian artist who has had a fantastic career in the West. His designs for the MTV Video Music Awards, a multimillion dollar production of *The Ring Cycle* in Amsterdam, and sets for *War and Peace* in Saint Petersburg and New York have all been spectacles of the highest class, major international events. In the context of the myth of the Russian avant-garde artist, such success is excessive and inconvenient: the true Russian artist should be destitute, lonely, and misunderstood. So it is evident that Tsypin is essentially more American than Russian (he stopped being Russian long ago), that what he specializes in is showmanship, and that the world of show has its own special laws: for an event to be successful, it has to be blown up out of proportion—which implies an emphasis on the superficial, on promotion, and on appeal to mass taste. The quality of a spectacle can easily be determined by whether it shatters all prior ideas held by the critics.

If your knowledge of Tsypin's life story has led you to form opinions about him, forget them—and look at things clearly. As everyone knows very well, theater is long dead. It was killed off by cinema, which in turn was killed off by television, while television was killed off by computers. Each successive killer makes more real—and more unbelievable—the space in which the action takes place. Entering the space, we come closer and closer to being magicians: we walk over water, fly through the air, even turn the sun on and off as we want. And just how can theater—with its sham and tawdry display of cardboard clouds suspended on ropes—compete with these technical wonders?

Tsypin manages to create theatrical spaces that make this magical technology seem like children's toys. If he could mass-produce what he does, it would be the end of cinema, television, and computers. In Tsypin's productions—as in *The*

Ring Cycle in Amsterdam—the orchestra flies over the audience, the audience flies over the stage, and the stage flies over the audience. Light turns into matter that can be inhaled and in which it is possible to fly, swim, and walk; glass, metal, and water come alive and flicker, waiting for the magician to wave his wand and give them final form. The screen of human consciousness—like St. Francis's gigantic screen of consciousness in the Salzburg production of Olivier Messiaen's opera—turns out to be capable of transforming the landscape. And all this is a hundred times more powerful than anything in film because it happens in real three-dimensional space, where you continue to feel the weight of your own body and the passing of time continues to be measured by the rhythm of your breathing.

I realize only too well that when you write about the modern artist you should use terms that belong to discourse on the latest tendencies in art. In Tsypin's case there is good reason to do so: his stage design is very close to current neomodern and (even more so) deconstructivist architecture. This link, however, says more about today's architecture—and its inclination for theatricality and spectacle—than it does about Tsypin. Major works do not necessarily show the influence of the latest pictures in fashionable magazines; they may have deep roots in history. His flying constructions and his chaotic geometry of planes, lines, and parabolas display the shadow of Russian constructivism. His stage design gives the impression that Vsevolod Meyerhold's theater did not end with the Stalinist shootings but continued to live, absorbing modern technology and assimilating the achievements of postwar art from pop art (the head of the *Statue of Liberty* in Vladimir Tatlin's tower at the MTV Video Music Awards) to deconstructivism (in *Biblical Pieces*).

But this similarity is only part of the picture. When it comes down to it, Tsypin's every line, plane, and spot of light works in a fashion that is utterly alien to constructivism. Constructivism moved toward things. As far as it was concerned, things did not mean anything and had no desire to mean anything; they simply were. The rigid structures of constructivist scenery were a new space, but not a space that was alive to the subject matter of the drama occurring within it.

Consider for example Alexander Vesnin's stage set for *The Man Who Was Thursday*. Vesnin created a multilevel transparent structure made of scaffolding, parts of which revolved and parts of which projected outward at a sharp diagonal angle. The projecting verticals prefigured the antennae of future constructivist buildings, while actors declaiming on the upper levels of the structure foreshadowed future monuments to revolutionary leaders. Together, this added up to a vivid image of the new world formed following the Russian Revolution. And yet when you examine the play itself—based on a novel by G. K. Chesterton—you find it has nothing at all to do with post-Revolutionary thought. On the contrary, its subject is how the English resisted an incipient revolution and prevented its horror. Which is to say that the logic of the action and the logic of the space in which this action occurs are not only out of sync with each other, but actually convey directly contradictory ideas.

In Tsypin's work everything is the other way around. He works not toward things, but away from them. When he brings metal and concrete onto the stage, it is not to create the image of a new world. Rather, he wants this metal and concrete to take on the role of actor, fill up with meaning, and acquire the power of movement, like a human being. He mostly designs stages for opera, and his work has a quality that is akin to musical phrasing: it comes from the resonance of extremely generalized matter expressing a thought, emotion, or mood. One of his installations, Earth Center for the Millennium Project in London, is structured around a display of the four primary elements of which the universe is made—water, air, earth, and fire. It is in this ancient, Pythagorean way—as heroes in a dramatic reenactment of the creation of the world—that Tsypin gets his materials and matter to perform on his stage sets.

This is something different from the constructivist way of understanding the nature of a production. I will even take the risk of characterizing it as symbolist. I think it is highly symptomatic that Tsypin's most important work, at least in terms of scale, has been Richard Wagner's *The Ring Cycle*. The Wagnerian concept of *Gesamtkunstwerk*—an aggregate artistic product that transforms space, matter, and life into a kind of solemn rite of the creation of the world—best applies to what Tsypin does on stage. Historically, the relationship between symbolism and the Russian avant-garde (and it is these, the most fertile strata of Russian art, that come to life in Tsypin's work) was marked by intense conflict. Between them came the Revolution, which explains why the avant-garde rejected symbolism as something to jettison from the steamship of modernity. There is only one other artist—from an utterly different field in art—in whom symbolism and the avant-garde likewise merged to form a single poetics, and that is Wasilly Kandinsky. Incidentally, it is my belief that had Kandinsky worked in theater, we would have had from him a very similar kind of stage design. In his abstractions matter is similarly material and immaterial simultaneously, similarly permeated with a meaning that is both highly abstract and highly profound, and similarly rich in musical and existential intonations.

I have already said that Tsypin works as if Stalin had not wiped out Meyerhold's theater. I should also say that he works as if there had never been any rift between the Russian avant-garde and constructivism, as if one had been the organic continuation of the other. His work offers us an alternative version of the history of Russian art in the twentieth century, one in which the fate of *Gesamtkunstwerk* took a comic turn. It is unlikely that Wagner or Vyacheslav Ivanov, who dreamed of theurgic art that would transform the city, could have imagined the possibility of fascist communist demonstrations based on their recipes. This was a tragedy, but it turned into a comedy with rock concerts that gather truly huge crowds where all are in the grip of one emotion, one rhythm, one word (a comedy because it is difficult to imagine Wagner and Ivanov as passionate defenders of rock music).

When you consider the way that the idea evolved, you cannot help being struck by the unfairness of this evolution. How did it come about that ideas that belonged to the avant-garde moved away from the latter into mass culture—which, for all its primitiveness, possesses an enormously attractive energy—while the avant-garde itself moved into galleries, where few ever look at it or where, if they do look, they have no inkling of what it is all about? In my view, Tsypin's stage design does something to amend this unfairness. In his work avant-garde ideas return to their natural environment, to an enormously energetic and large-scale attempt to transform reality into magic reality. We can justifiably feel a little proud that Russian constructivism and symbolism have made this comeback on the world stage, and in the work of a Russian artist—even if Tsypin is not altogether Russian, but a Russian American. Which perhaps is for the best: at any rate, Tsypin is not bound by the myth of the Russian artist as incomprehensible, superfluous, and a failure.

Act I
WATER REFLECTIONS

I often imagine a stage as a subterranean vault, a cavernous dungeon flooded with water, something dripping from the ceiling, rotting walls covered in moss, with putrid air that smells of death. It is one of those semisubmerged basements in Venice or Amsterdam, or some forgotten storage space for old nineteenth-century sets in Saint Petersburg. This space is quiet, haunted by spirits, pregnant with the possibilities of myth, music, light, and the world itself—the room of innermost desire.

In this space I see women in childbirth, nymphs, maidens, fetuses, fountains, and cosmic discs. It is a primordial womblike space with a feminine emptiness, forever mysterious and forever unattainable. Water takes us back to our unconscious prenatal state. It is akin to our eyes, always moist and always moving.

We associate water with birth and death. I imagine a transparent gondola making the final journey into another world. A single ray of sunlight reveals a huge room reflected upside down, a bottomless well, a space suspended between the past and the future, Earth and heaven, the worlds of the living and of the dead. Maybe I need that reflective surface in order to expand the universe.

In his poem, "Bronze Horseman," Aleksander Pushkin introduces—in addition to the people and the Czar—a third, uncontrollable force: the flood. Flood here is an element of chaos, nature, God—ever lurking disaster. Andrei Bely picks up that theme: "From far, far away, as though farther off than they should have been, the islands sank and cowered in fright; and the buildings cowered; it seemed that the waters would sink and that at that instant the depths, the greenish murk would surge over them."[1]

For Kandinsky, however, the flood is a catastrophe, but a creation as well. It is the deep cosmic blue swallowing all of the forms and the universe itself. Gradually it takes on the shape of the ocean of consciousness as in Andrei Tarkovsky's *Solaris*. It is an enormous creative force out of which the first images are beginning to burst to life.

1   Andrei Bely, *Petersburg* (1922), trans. and ed. Robert A. Maguire and John E. Malmstad (Bloomington: Indiana University Press, 1978), 9.

Death in Venice

This opera is based on the novel by Thomas Mann. The set has the atmosphere of a ghostly, ephemeral, decaying city as seen in the mind of a dying man. In the first act, as he is wandering through the narrow streets, the glass and mirror panels—walls with fragments of windows and balconies—constantly shift and change perspective. Only a tiny vertical slit of unattainable sky remains still.

In the second act, the entire world of Venice collapses on its side. In the inflamed mind of the dying man, the facade of the building, a beach, and a hotel room merge into one delirious whole. All the characters/singers emerge from the windows/graves.

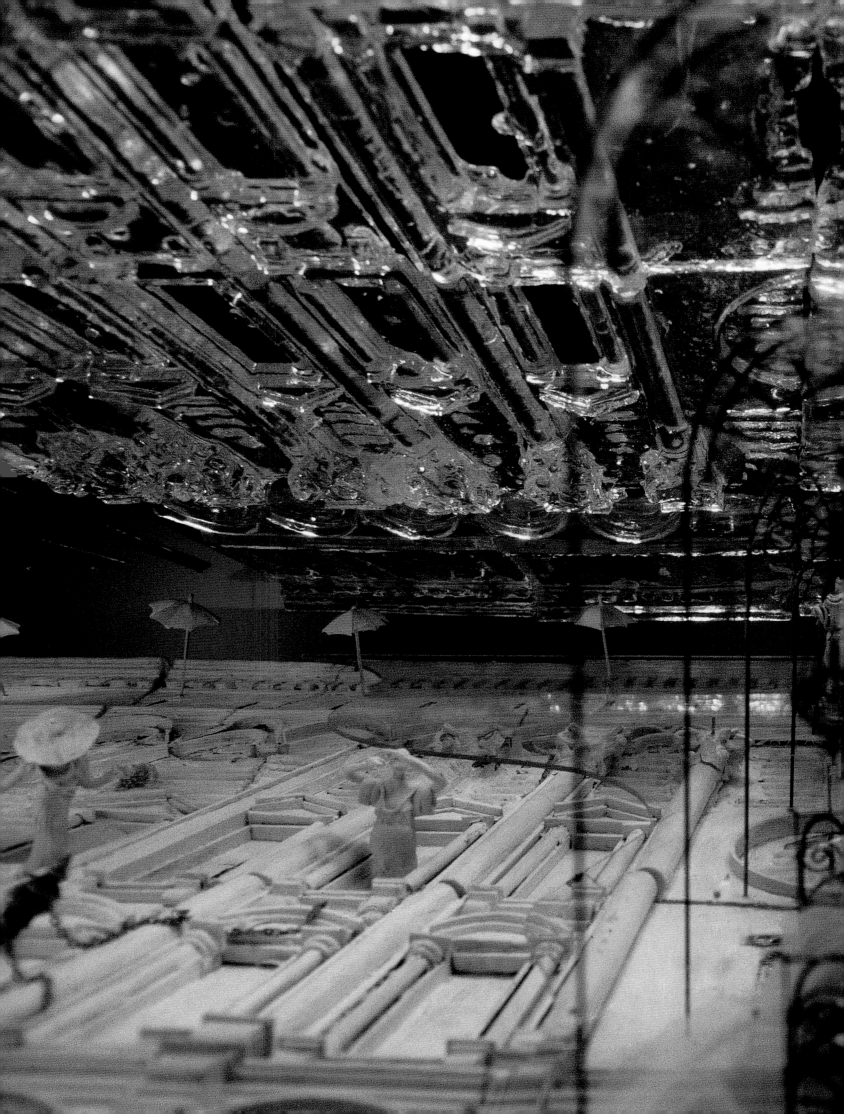

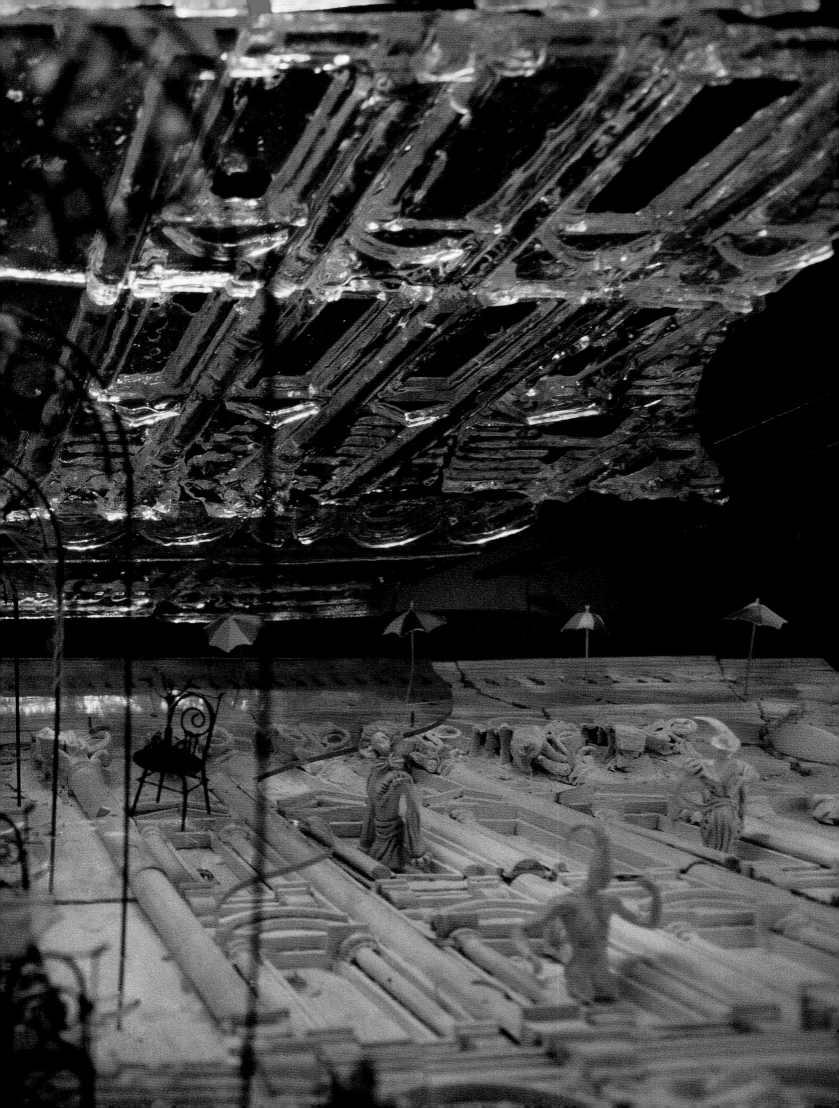

Oedipus Rex

Igor Stravinsky's short opera, *Oedipus Rex,* is an oratorio; a series of tableaux are interrupted by the narration of the story. With its enormous chorus, masks, puppets, and narrator, it was a monumental presentation of Sophocles's play. People look like sculptures and sculptures like people while masks make everyone look like ghosts: it is the world of the dead.

The set is a gigantic eye made of bent wood. In the middle of the space there is a floating disc that moves in different directions. Sometimes we see the spirit of Oedipus on it, sometimes his mother. On that disc Jocasta eventually commits suicide. The stage is a black lake with a floating wooden construction. It is surrounded by rocks made of wrinkled mosquito netting, which has a very three-dimensional yet eerie, ephemeral feeling. The rocks reflect in the water, creating a terrifying, bottomless well. The infrastructure looks at times like a mythic bird whose wings appear to move under the feet of the chorus. At others it looks like a strange spiderlike animal. The place seems mysterious, sick, and cursed.

When Oedipus pokes his eyes out, the entire surrounding mountain disappears as an enormous sweep of red silk is released from the flies. As a member of the audience, you feel your eyes are bloodied. In the next tableau, Oedipus and the chorus go into the underworld of the black water and ritual fire with the final tremendous music.

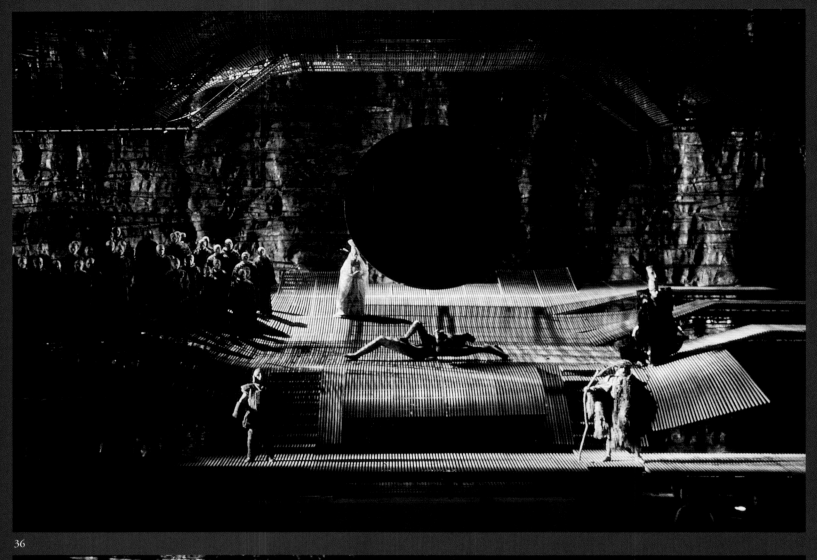

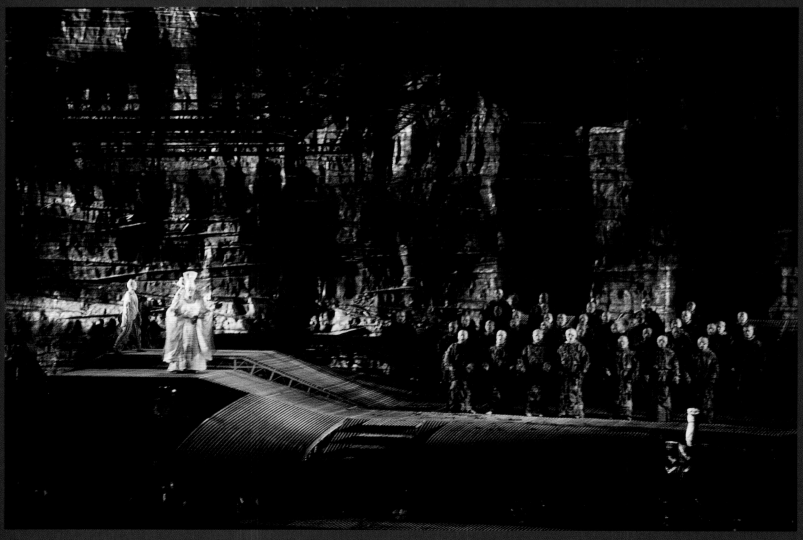

Boris Godunov

Boris Gudonov is the story of a man ruined by his guilty conscience. When he comes to power in the beginning of the opera, he is already only a shadow of a man. The audience is trapped inside his mind: mad, paranoid, and suspicious. Conceived right after September 11th during the height of anthrax hysteria, the opera has a strange resonance and immediacy. One of the many theories about Godunov's life suggests that he was dying of slow poisoning, and that his children were poisoned as well. It was this feeling—that everything around you, every surface, could be contaminated, toxic, and deadly—that I wanted to capture. The architecture itself seems to be organic, biomorphic, and alive.

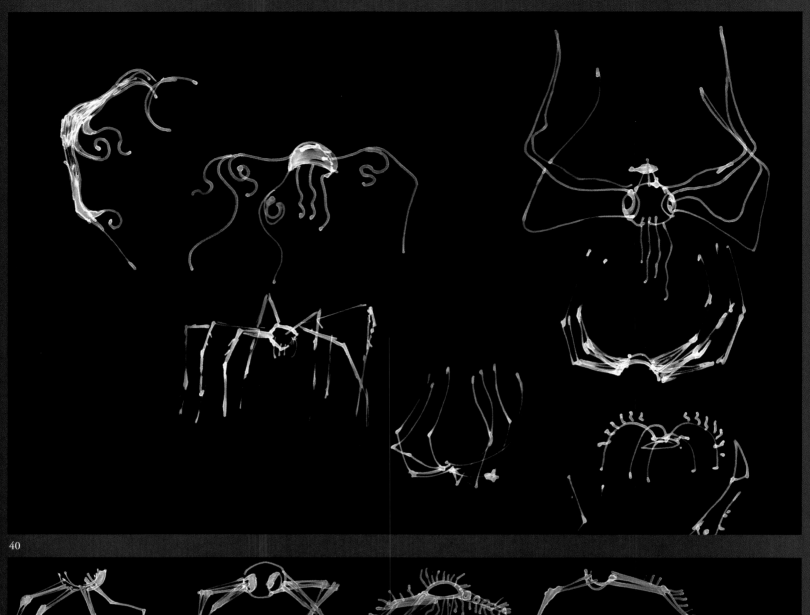

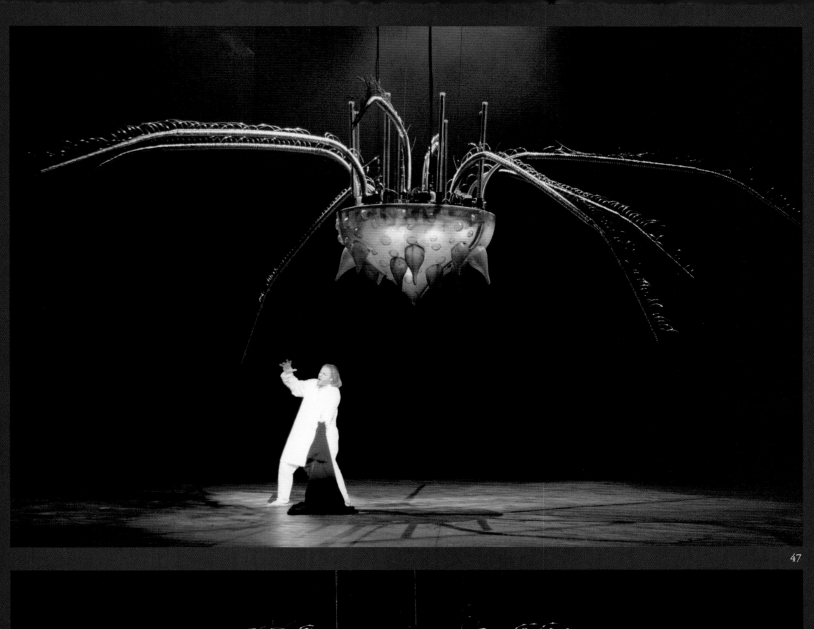

Russian Pavilion

The design for the Russian Pavilion at the Venice Biennale explored the tension between Saint Petersburg and Moscow, East and West, Russia and Europe, classical and modern architecture, the conscious and the subconscious.

The ground floor was the dark space of the stage, dreams, and imagination. Two rooms were flooded with black water, in the middle of which were two glass sculptures. The first was a boat with the familiar columns and fragments of Saint Petersburg architecture. The second was an endless glass spiral tower, reminiscent of Tatlin's tower, with hundreds of onion domes lit with fiber optics floating in the water: that was Moscow. The dark brooding music, slowly changing lights, and wildly swinging light bulbs created a metaphor of the stormy journey of Russian architecture and of Russian history itself.

The upper floor was devoted to two projects: the reconstruction of the Bolshoi Theater, which represented the conservative preservation of the past, and the design for the new Mariinsky Theater by Eric Owen Moss, a bold breakthrough into the future. I divided the two with a broken glass wall, with the shards of glass frozen in space as if enormous meteorites had crashed into the wall. This was the effect of Moss's design on Russian architecture. The wall also points to Saint Petersburg as the broken remains of Peter the Great's "Window to the West."

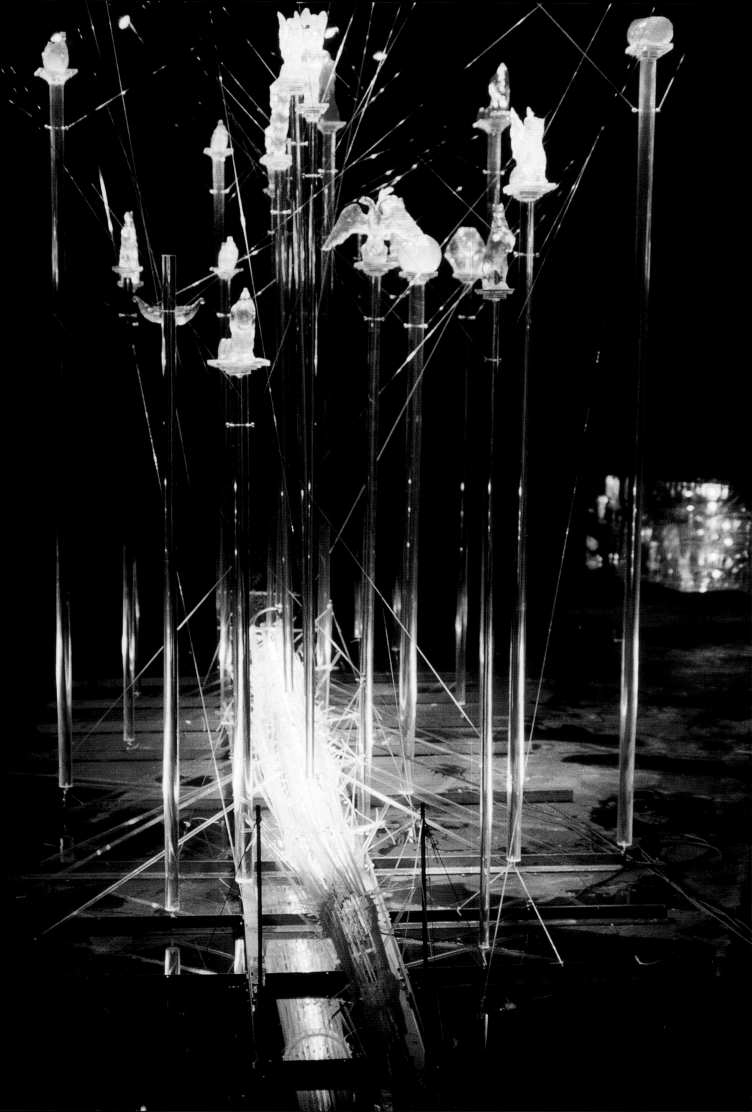

L'Amour de Loin

L'Amour de Loin is the story of a medieval poet who is in love with a princess whom he has never seen. He lives in the West, and she is in the East. He writes poems to her and delivers them via a pilgrim. Finally, he gathers the courage to go on a journey to see her. He gets sick during his trip across the sea, and he dies just as he sees her for the first time. The stage is flooded with water. On either side of the stage, there are two endless glass towers dissolving into the sky, one for each character. The pilgrim travels back and forth between them by glass boat.

The set actually tells the whole story. In the first act, the two main characters move only vertically, confined to narrow towers that can fit only one person each. When the poet finds the courage to leave his glass tower and steps into the water, it becomes a terrifying moment visually, dramatically, and musically. The final aria is sung by the princess as she lies in the water, while the whole theater dissolves in shimmering, dancing reflections.

Pelléas et Mélisande

The action of the opera takes place in a California-style house overhanging a mountain—half hospital, half modern office, a nightmare of deconstructivist architecture. Each character is trapped in his or her own room. The set becomes a metaphor for the modern American family, while the house itself is the symbol of alienation and emptiness of the soul. The ocean below was made with hundreds of fluorescent bulbs, flickering with different colors like the reflection of a distant city in the water.

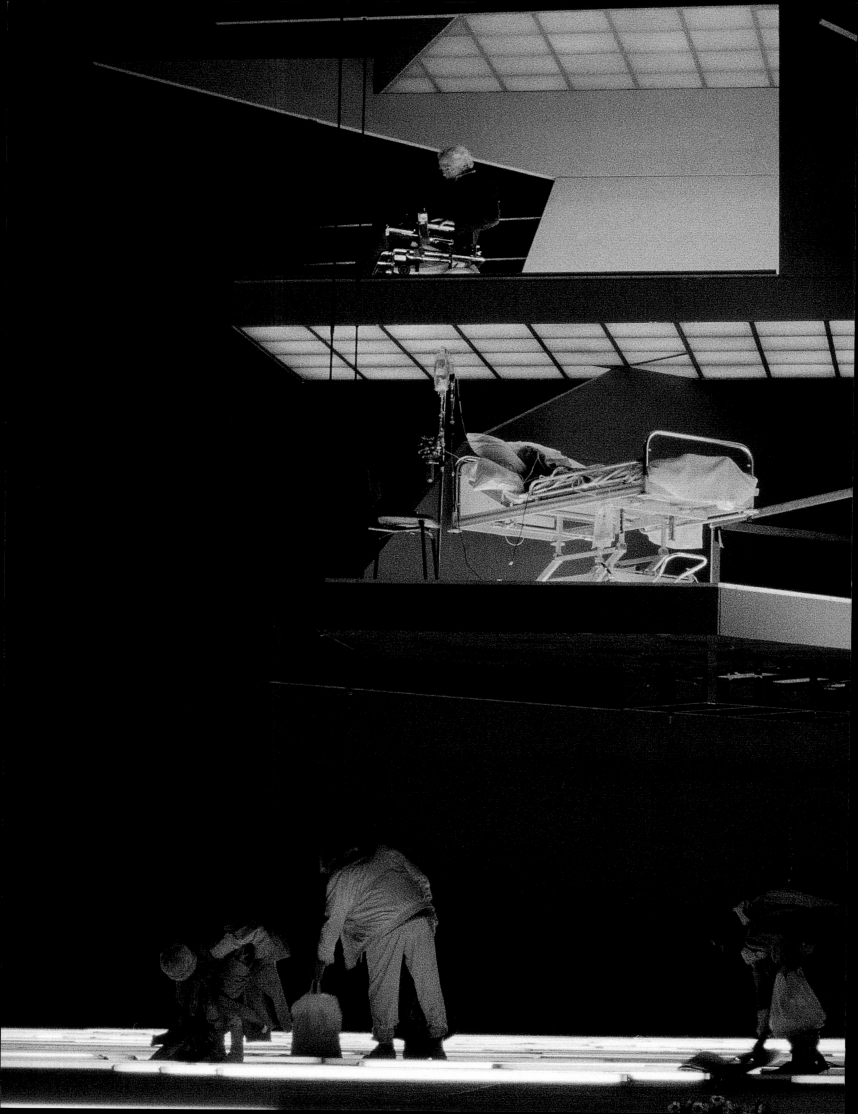

West Side Story

I do not know from where the image of a collapsed skyscraper came. I think I felt that the skyscraper is the symbol of New York and, in fact, of America, but I needed to create a stage, a playing area, and a dance floor. So I kept drawing the skyscraper sideways, down into the water, to create a horizontal surface. Yet I needed a vertical thrust as well. I was looking for the image of a society at the heart of which something is broken.

Eventually the nightmarish vision I had in the middle of the night was actually calculated by a team of engineers and built by a real construction company specializing in glass-and-steel office buildings and skyscrapers. I used glass that matched the color of the water so that the whole sculpture became a crystallized wave. It was a building that seemed to be on the verge of falling and rising at the same time—a symbol of America. At the top, there is a dreamlike, transparent vision of Manhattan, always distant and unattainable. It is another world, perhaps the only shelter for the people in the musical. "There's a place for us. Somewhere..."

As a contrast to this gleaming corporate structure, there is a fragment of a brick tenement building, a church, a liquor store, and a bridal shop all at once. It moves on subway tracks and it seems as if it could fall into the water any minute. This is the world of immigrants on the move, out of place as eternal outsiders.

I presented the model six months before September 11th. Afterwards, all of a sudden, the design took on a whole new, much more ominous meaning. We realized, however, that there was no going back, that this in a way was a much more authentic image of New York now. And we knew that the meaning of September 11th and *West Side Story* is the same: people are killed only because they are different.

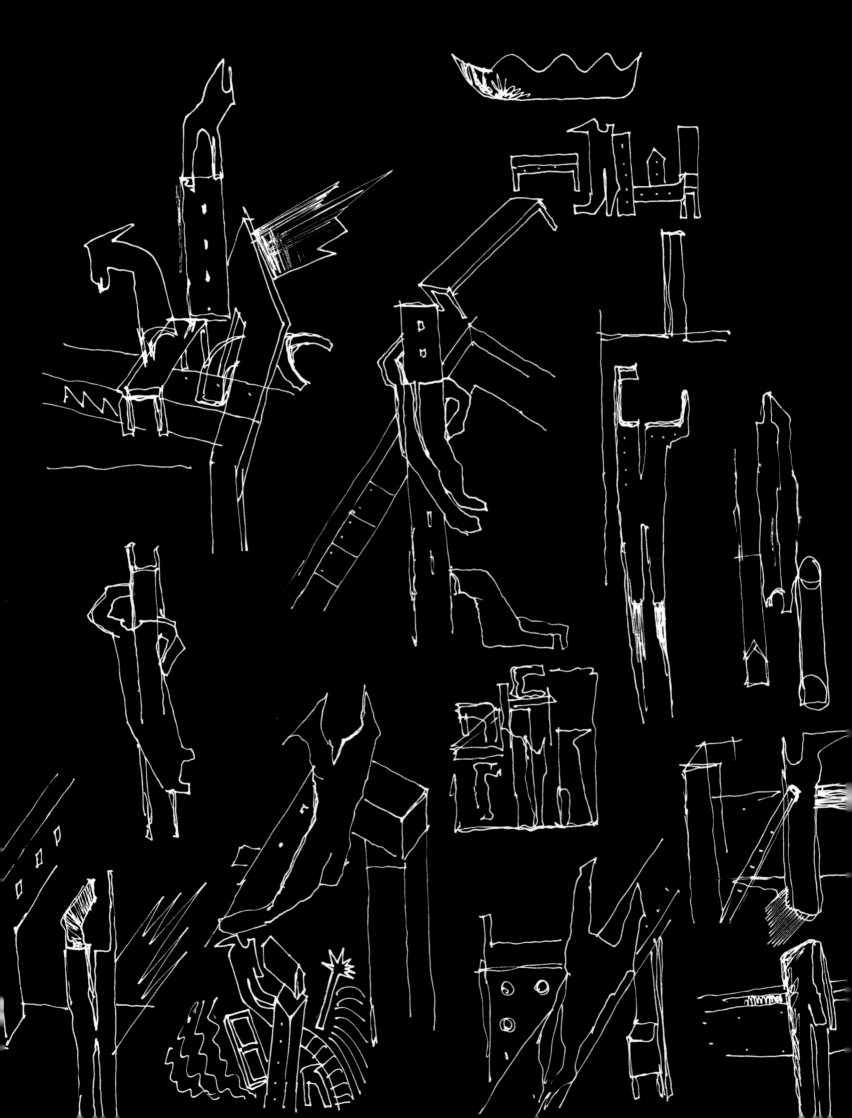

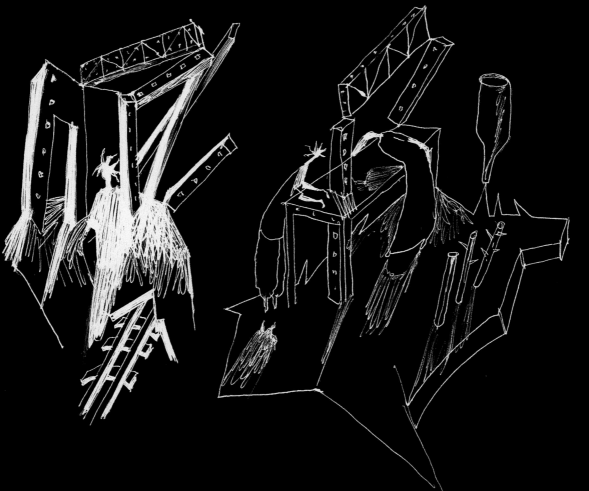

Act II

ALL THAT IS SOLID MELTS INTO AIR

In theater there is nothing more powerful than space. Today, when movies, television, and computers—all flat projections on a screen—dominate our visual world, theater uniquely takes place in three dimensions. Many architects of the Russian avant-garde designed for the stage in the early twentieth century. In fact, stage sets were often their only realized constructions. They used the theater as a lab for new ideas. In a Russian context, theater is always at the center of culture. Their discoveries not only laid out the foundations of modern scenography, but often inspired new architecture as well.

Meanwhile, their descendents, the deconstructivists—such as Frank Gehry, Daniel Libeskind, and Zaha Hadid—are attracted by the mystery and spiritual dimension of designing for the stage. All are getting involved in major opera projects. There is a connection that has been building for years between contemporary architecture and stage design. As architecture tends towards the ephemeral, the temporary, and the kinetic, it is read more as entertainment and advertisement. As buildings become events more than static monuments, they will one day be said to be "directed" by an architect. Architects who are able to come up with big theatrical metaphors usually win competitions. In my work, I try to find the most powerful and complete expression of these two tendencies.

The sets I design seem too big for the stage; they seem to burst through the walls. They are in constant clash with the architecture that is supposed to enclose them. They are in the process of destruction and rebuilding at the same time, as if the design itself is an attempt to break through into another world. The sets I design are antitheatrical, inflexible, and awkward—architectural compositions frozen in time. The tension of the space unrelenting, as if time has stopped and you have entered a different realm where horizontal movement of time and narrative is no longer possible. One has to move vertically on the path of consciousness.

Vertical is the most important direction in opera. Vertical is spiritual. Vincent Van Gogh painted trees that were higher than the stars. He said that they communicated to him an ambition to reach the cosmos. I was told that I am a wood element according to Chinese alchemy. Wood is flexible but strong, and as a tree it never stops expanding upward. It is a challenge in opera to take the action off the floor. Singers love the floor; they need the certainty of the floor to produce their sound. And yet when you manage to raise the chorus off the floor there is a soaring airborne effect. In theater you can defeat gravity. All energy goes upward. Things fly. Very heavy things fly.

In Russian icons, the saints are surrounded by surreal, illogical architecture. Some people think that icon painters just did not know perspective. But if you study these icons more closely you realize that their creators could not paint such an intricate architecture by accident. This nonsensical space shows the otherworldly character of what is happening in the world of the saints. Once you abandon rational, illustrative, or literal space, you begin to reach for its spiritual dimension.

In Japanese military arts, warriors abandon the rational mind in order to allow them to anticipate their rival's every move. When two masters are fighting, it becomes a ballet, theoretically without an end. Each one operates on pure intuition. Something similar happens as I let my hands sculpt the space in a model.

For me, design is the search for the sculptural melody of the space, whereas sculpture explores form. The two—design and sculpture—feed on each other. Sculpture in a way is building a model without the constraints of real theatrical space; instead it tries to capture the "other space" that is implied in theater but often remains in the imagination. For me, the model itself is a very autonomous work of art. It has to have an integrity of its own. When building a sculpture or a model, I use glass, steel, wood, and stones. My sculptures seem to be inhabited by invisible people or strange mythical creatures. But they are not there: they will show up later...on stage.

In viewing my work, I want the audience to experience the vertiginous sensation akin to traveling up the spiral of Vladimir Tatlin's Monument to the Third International. Its architecture is an ultimate realization of cathedral art, an invention of the Russian avant-garde implying a mass gathering and collective consciousness on a global scale. With its spiral shape thrusting upward piercing the sky, it is a perfect vision of crystallized spirit. But its kinetic power, akin to the movement of a bolt of lighting, represents much more: the actual transformation of human consciousness.

Saint Francis of Assisi

My first influence on this design came from Assisi itself. Driving up the mountains approaching Assisi is the most unforgettable experience. The city seems completely unattainable—you are not sure whether the vision is real. Then all of a sudden a breathtaking 360-degree panorama opens up and you have reached the peak. You are exhausted, the vertigo makes you nauseous, the sky is psychedelic, the landscape is hallucinatory. That is the atmosphere I wanted to capture in this production. When I say atmosphere, I do not mean enormous backdrops or Styrofoam mountains. I mean the feeling of being at the edge of this world, the feeling of being allowed a glimpse of another world.

The stage set is a cathedral in the process of being built or being destroyed—exploding, crashing through the mountain, flying into the cosmos. The inspirations here are icons, the structure of Gothic cathedrals, Russian constructivism, and the freedom of dreaming in space. The wooden floor and the cliff are stylized with jagged lines, as in Byzantine painting. The dominance of untreated, bare wood overall is shocking. It makes you think of the cross, of the naked body of Christ. And on top of this is a square structure of thousands of fluorescent lights constantly changing patterns and color. They are pulsing, vulgar, impossible, sickening—creating a sky of the inflamed mind inspired by medieval illuminated manuscripts. Scenes are played with little constructions made of television sets that become little caves, rooms, churches, and coffins.

78

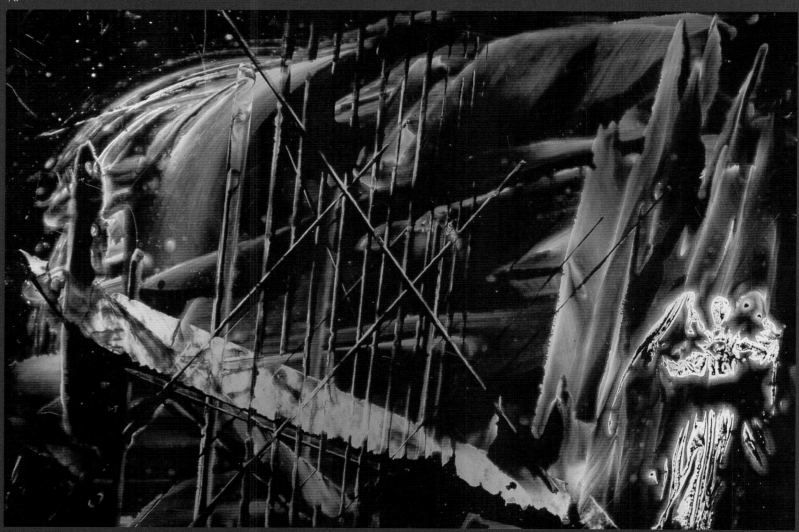

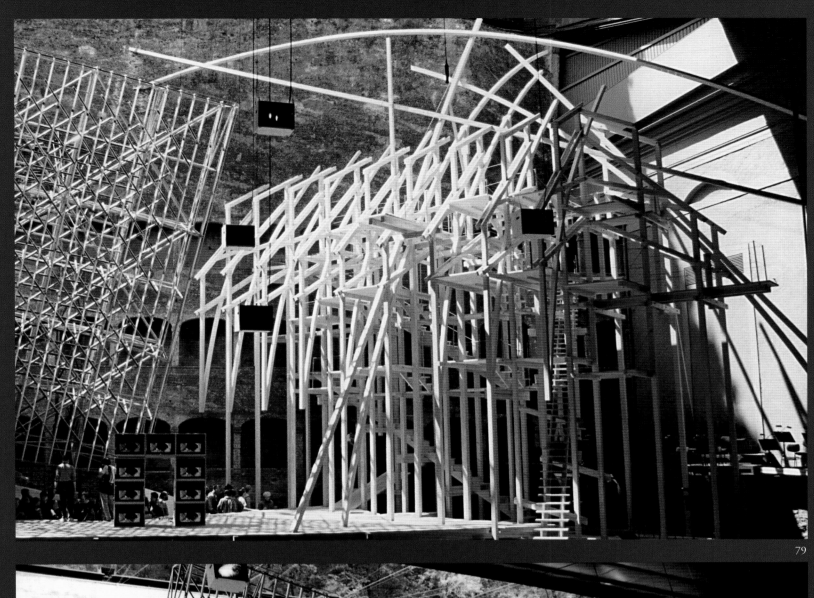

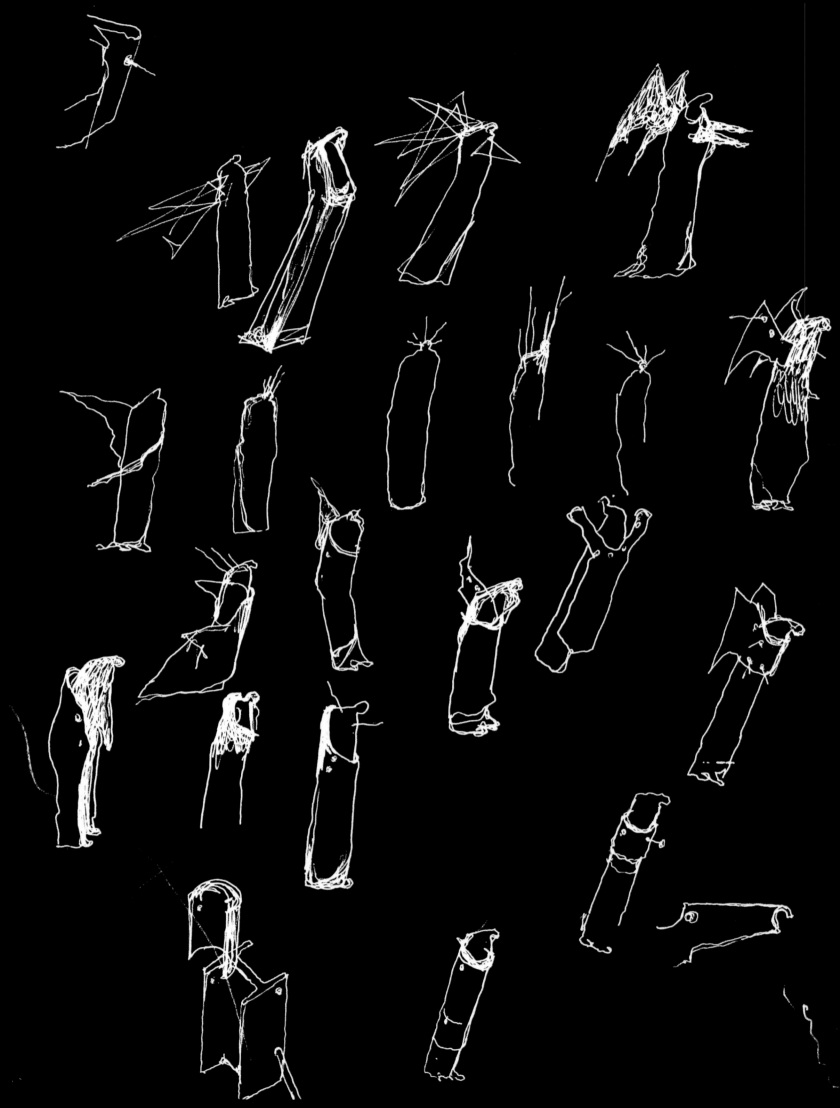

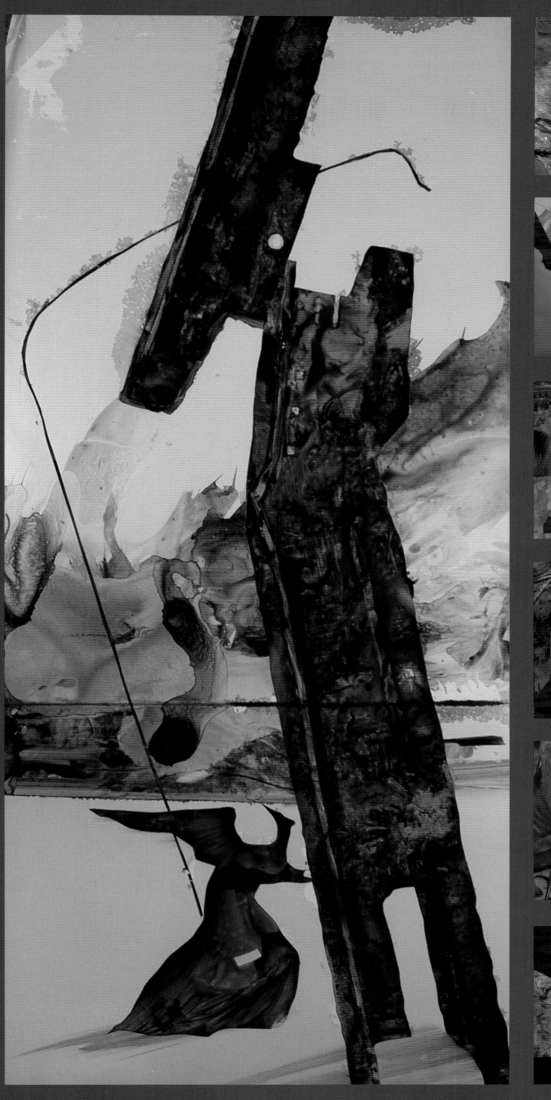

81

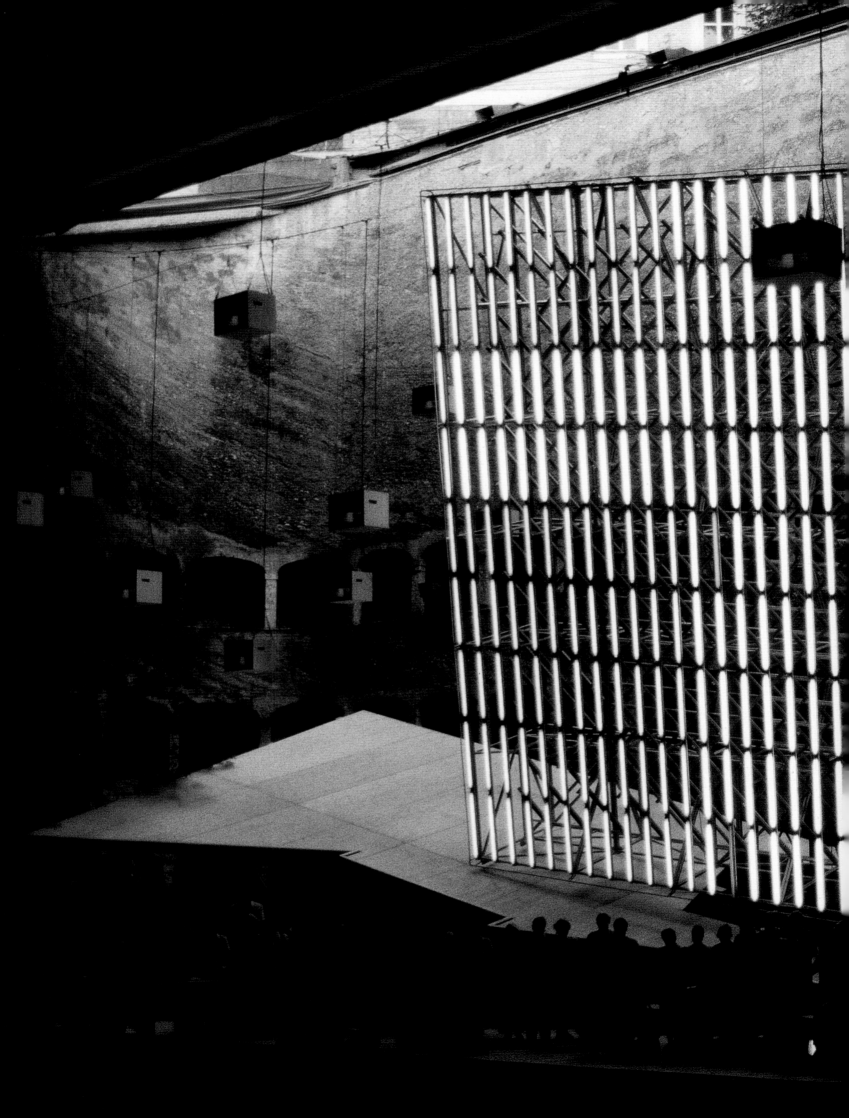

Biblical Pieces

In dealing with biblical stories, I knew that whatever I tried to literally visualize on stage would look trivial and inadequate. The only language I could use was music, sculpture, and dance. My idea then was to rethink the orchestra, spatially. The typical way the orchestra is laid out is very rigid and determined by the sound of the composition. It is almost impossible to tamper with it, let alone completely reconceive its whole spatial arrangement vertically.

I wanted to make the orchestra into a collapsing Tower of Babel, an ark, a biblical tree, and a rock in the desert at the same time. Fresh exposed wood became the sand, the desert sky, and ultimately, in the last section, the body of Christ. Long floating boats pierced and destroyed the tower with enormous fluorescent tubes so that lightning became the materialized voice of God's wrath.

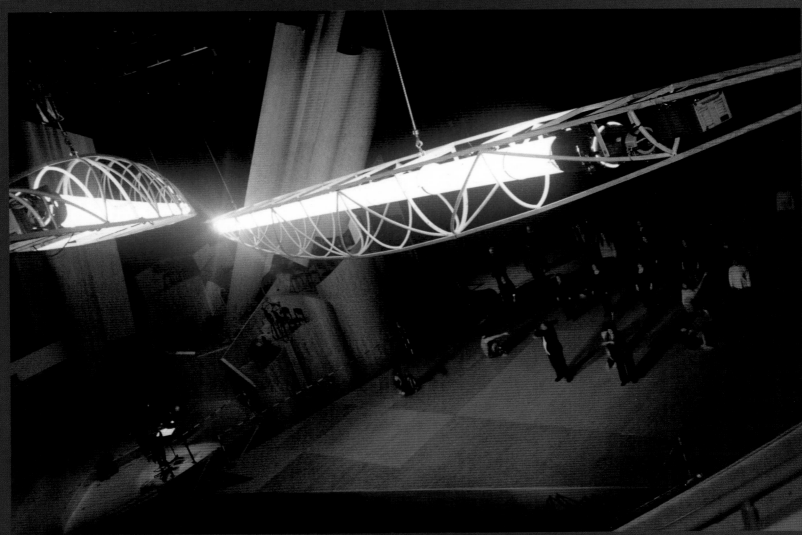

MTV Video Music Awards

The MTV set was Vladimir Tatlin's Monument to the Third International transfixed by the *Statue of Liberty*. The upcoming end of the century influenced this design. I took the image of the Russian Revolution that took place at the beginning of the century and juxtaposed it with the symbol of New York, the symbol of urbanization, the apotheosis of the twentieth century. I included falling skyscrapers as recognizable features of the city skyline. (We had problems with this; the silhouette of the Chrysler Building is copyrighted, and so it had to be removed.)

Many designs that I do are filmed and I am accustomed to seeing them through a television camera. When I build a model, we film it from every angle. It has to work both as a general picture and in the details. The spiral on MTV was conceived for a low camera, like those used when they shoot with a wide angle from below. It worked very well.

Millennium Cities

Fifteen-meter-high shards of glass were used as the image of cities of the future. The impact of urbanization was shown through the layers of earth, industrial waste, pollution, plants, and sky presented as layouts of stones, shells, leaves mixed with metal, and plastic junk attached to glass. Thus these shards became vertical sections through the entire ecosystem. They also served as enormous screens for video projections and slides, showing the images of traffic, endless skyscrapers, people, and smog. The sound and the music score reinforced the suffocating and claustrophobic effect of overurbanization.

The Ring Cycle (Amsterdam)

In *The Ring Cycle* in Amsterdam, the world explodes around the orchestra—the originator of sound, the main life force. Losing the pit as its anchor, the orchestra appears to be either onstage or so far in the house that you cannot distinguish between musicians and the audience. Some of the audience find themselves floating above the stage with elements of the set in the middle of the house, backstage, crushing against the walls, and piercing the ceiling and the floor. And the singers seem close, like a cinematic close-up, and then they reappear one hundred feet away, in a long shot. Your imagination takes you outside to the street, into the underworld, into space.

All four operas of *The Ring Cycle* are built on the idea of constructing the world out of primary materials. Medieval and alchemical imagery, the legends that inspired Wagner's understanding of creation, dictated my choice of materials for *Das Rheingold*. I created three enormous square platforms, constantly moving in space. Water and sky were made of glass, the earth was steel, and the mirrorlike, shimmering surface of brushed aluminum in the back suggests unattainable Valhalla. *Die Walküre* is a more sensual natural world where wood is the dominant material. A disk made of bent wood suggests the cut of a tree as well as the moon. The orchestra is cut into the disk and strange steel shapes are thrust into the tree: perhaps this is the sword left for Siegmund by Wotan? The world of *Siegfried* is even more twisted, complex, and schizophrenic. It's as if we have entered a magic forest. Its main road, seemingly made of one steel blade, at one point starts to move and wakes up as a dragon. And then, out of nowhere, the magic circle of fire surrounding Brunhilde appears, but this fire is made of glass, which here seems to become fire, water, and sky at different times. The design for the *Götterdämmerung*, the final opera of *The Ring Cycle*, is dominated by a kind of falling Tower of Babel. An endless stone beam hovers above the house and eventually crushes the glass floor. Then this floor rises as piles and piles of glass shards of ice to become the flood. Finally comes an image of burning Valhalla as flames completely surround the stage. And then thousands of fluorescent lights, unnoticed until now, light the audience, the balconies, and the entire theater. We feel the theater itself is on fire, that Valhalla is us. The circle is complete.

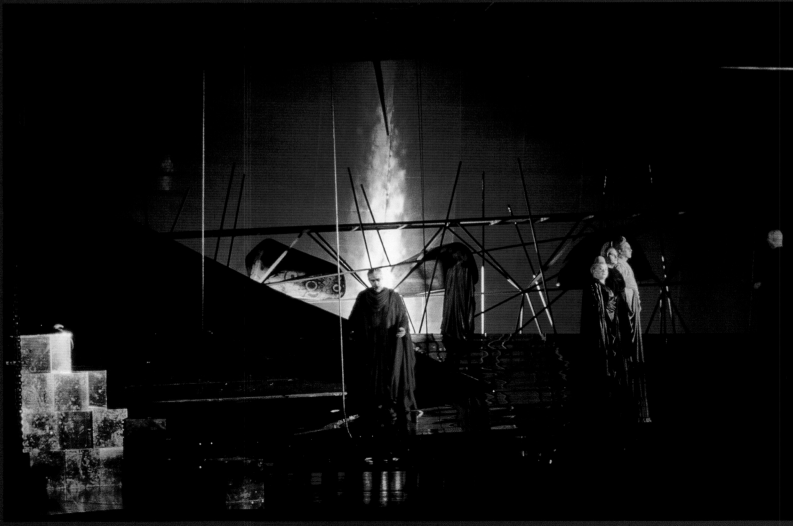

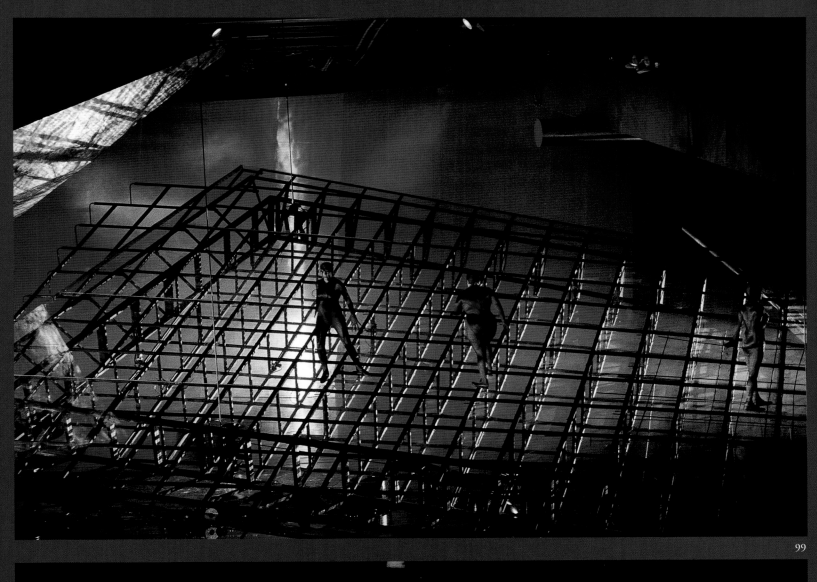

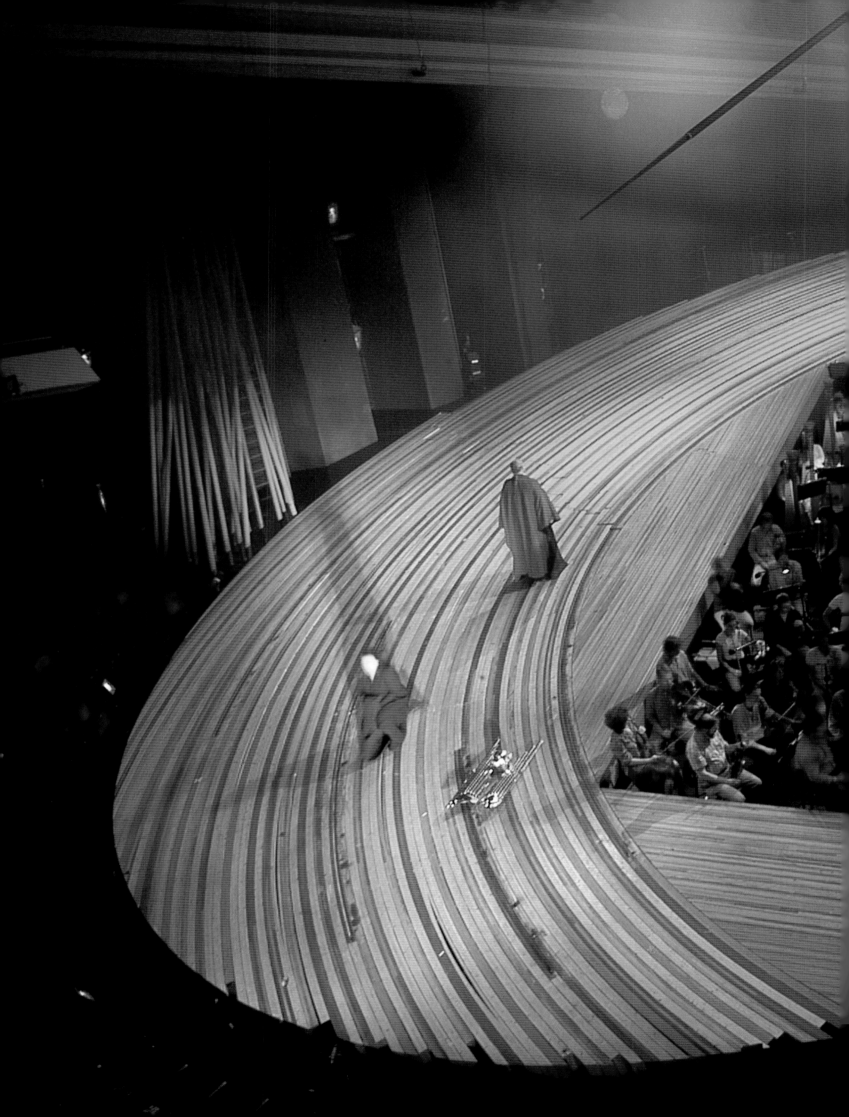

102

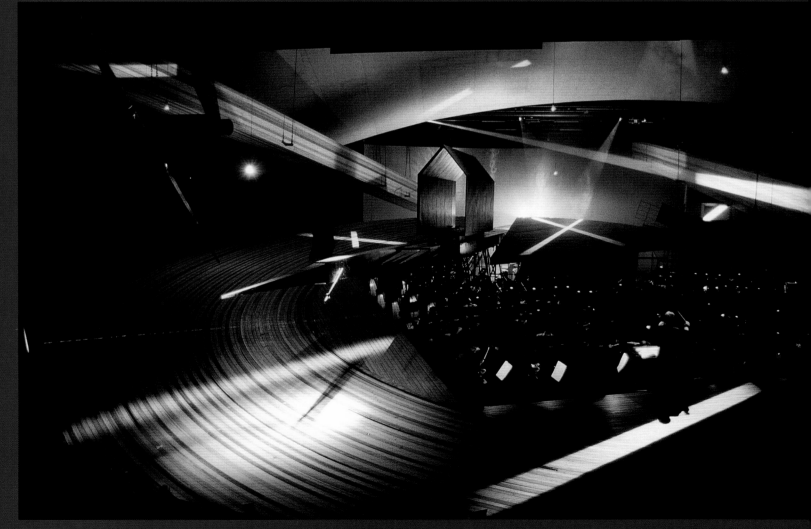

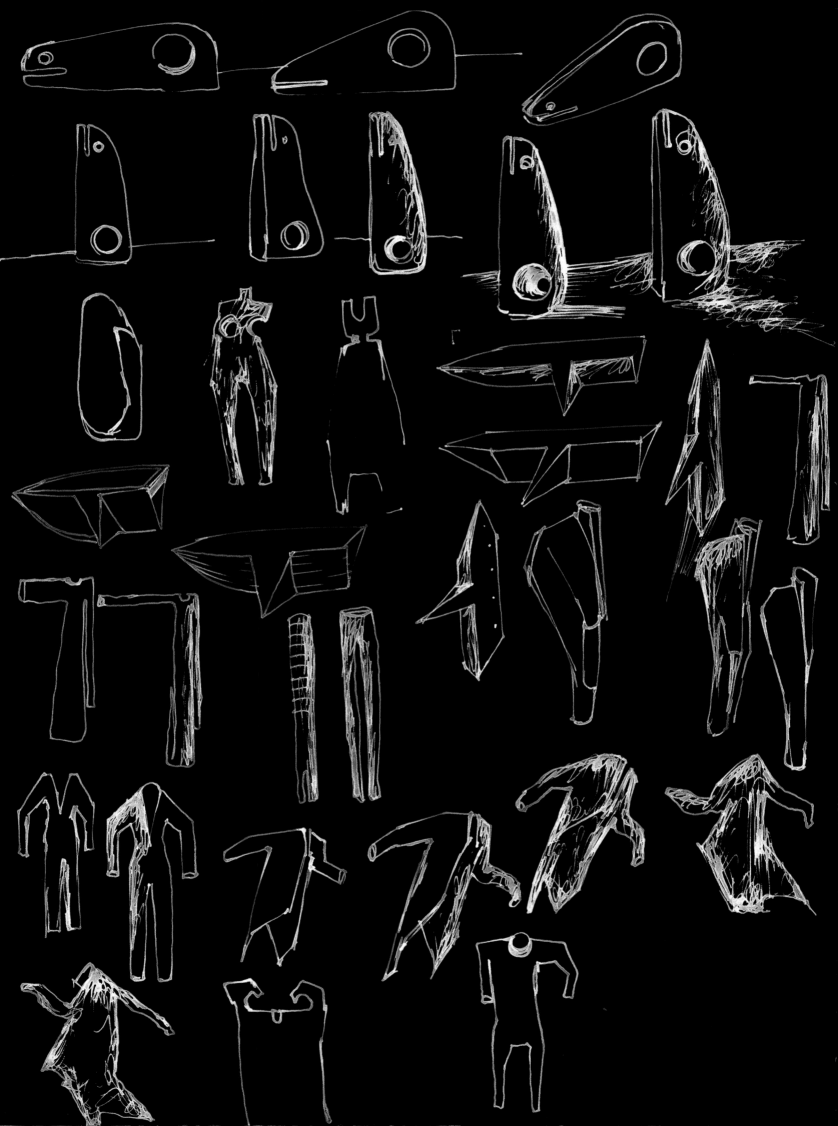

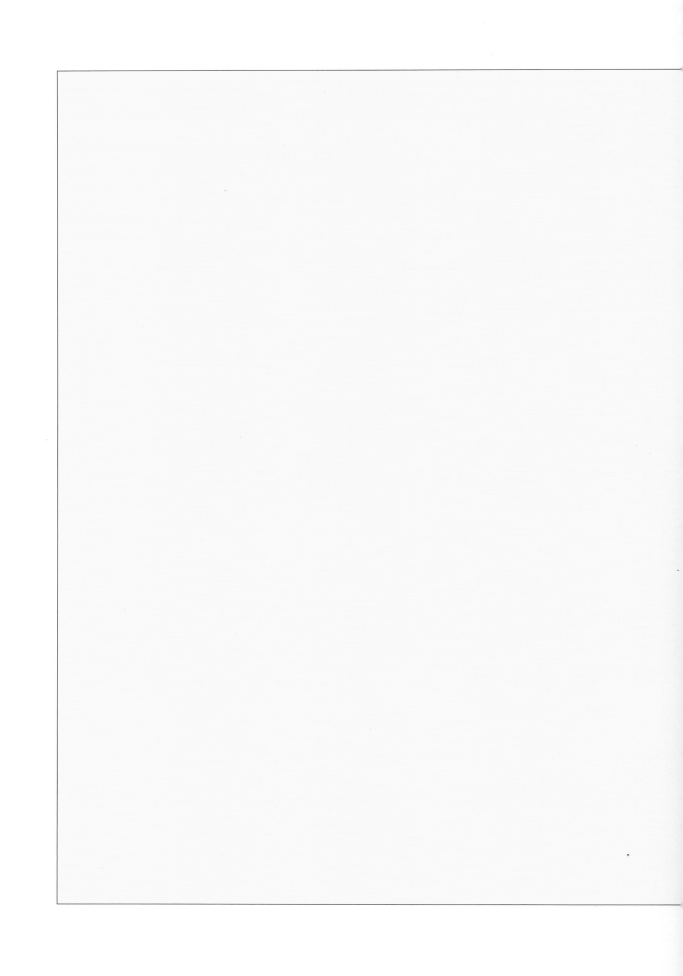

Interlude

Building an Endless Tower

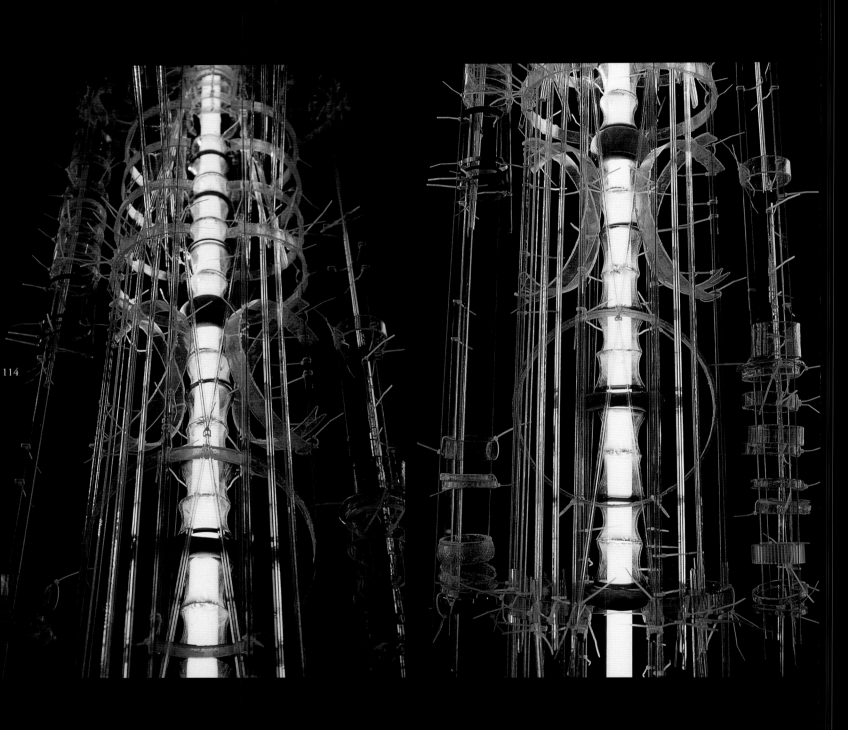

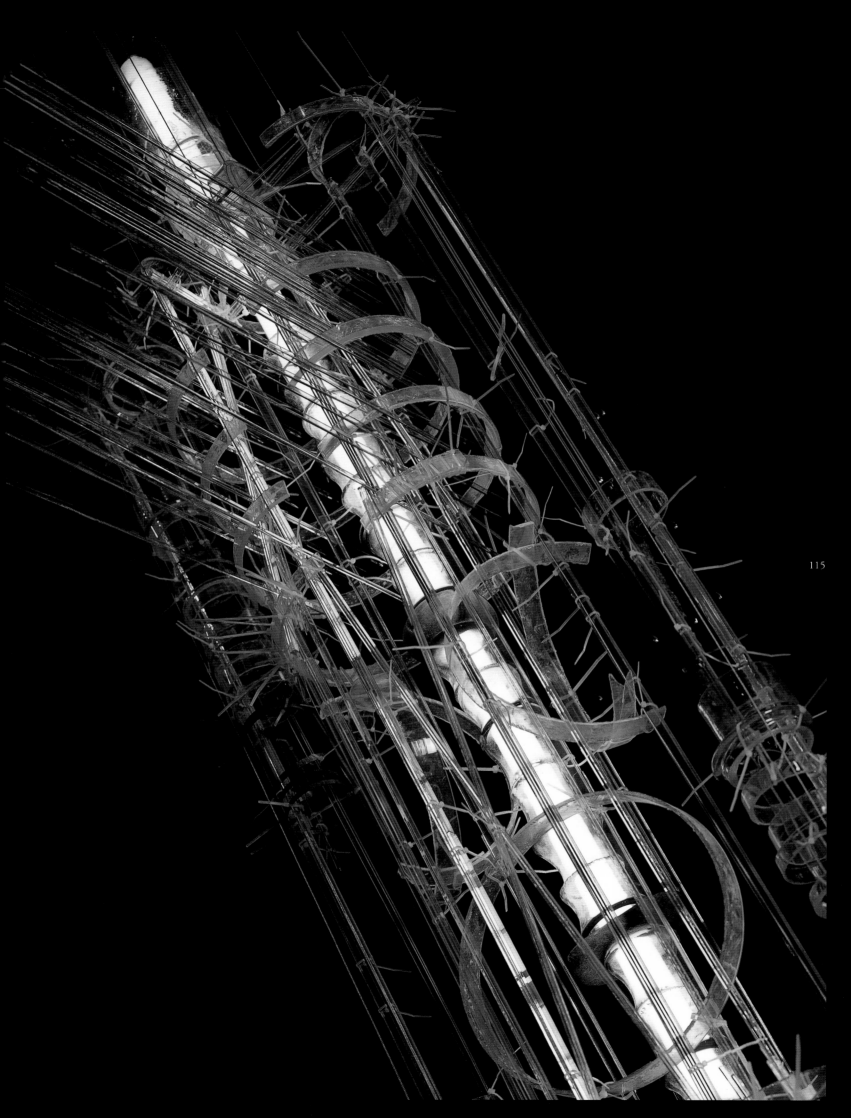

115

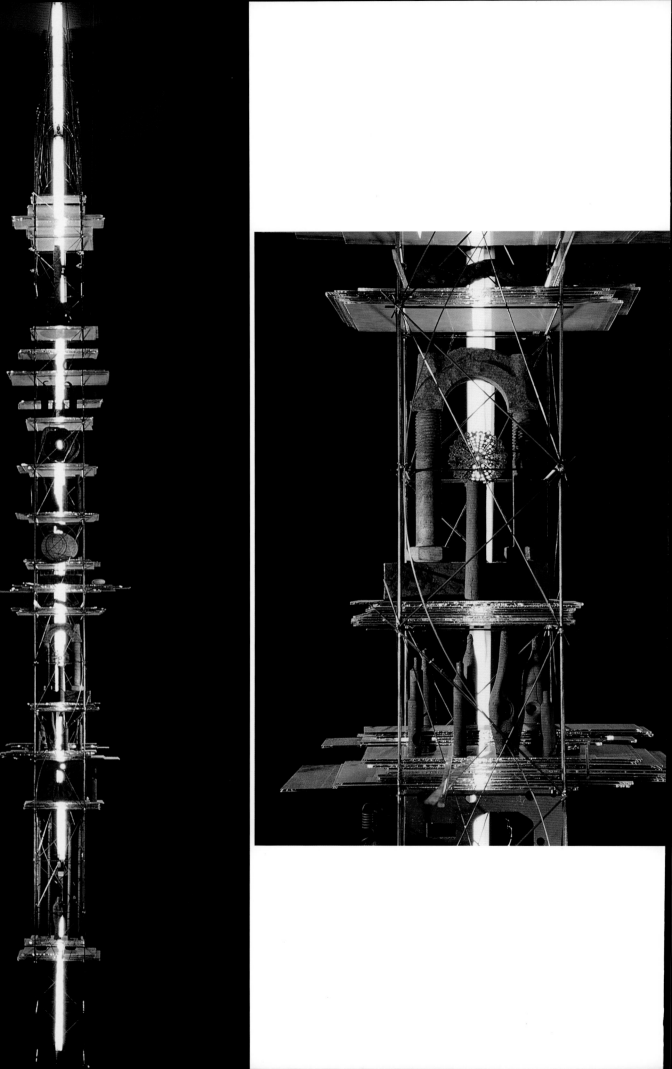

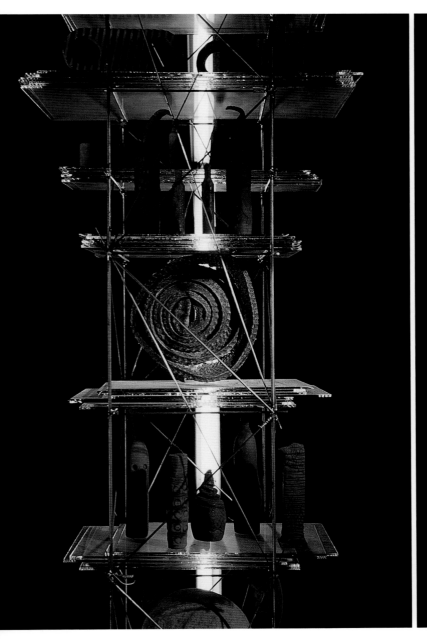

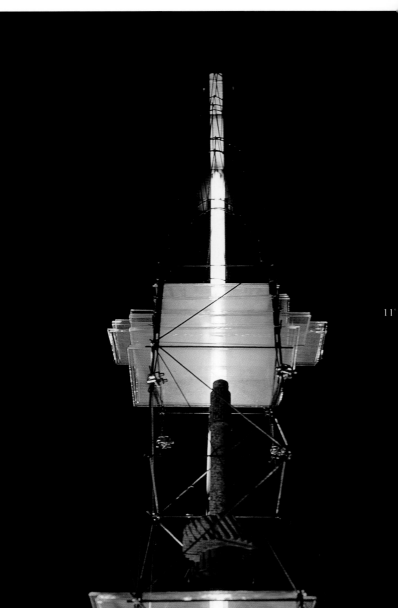

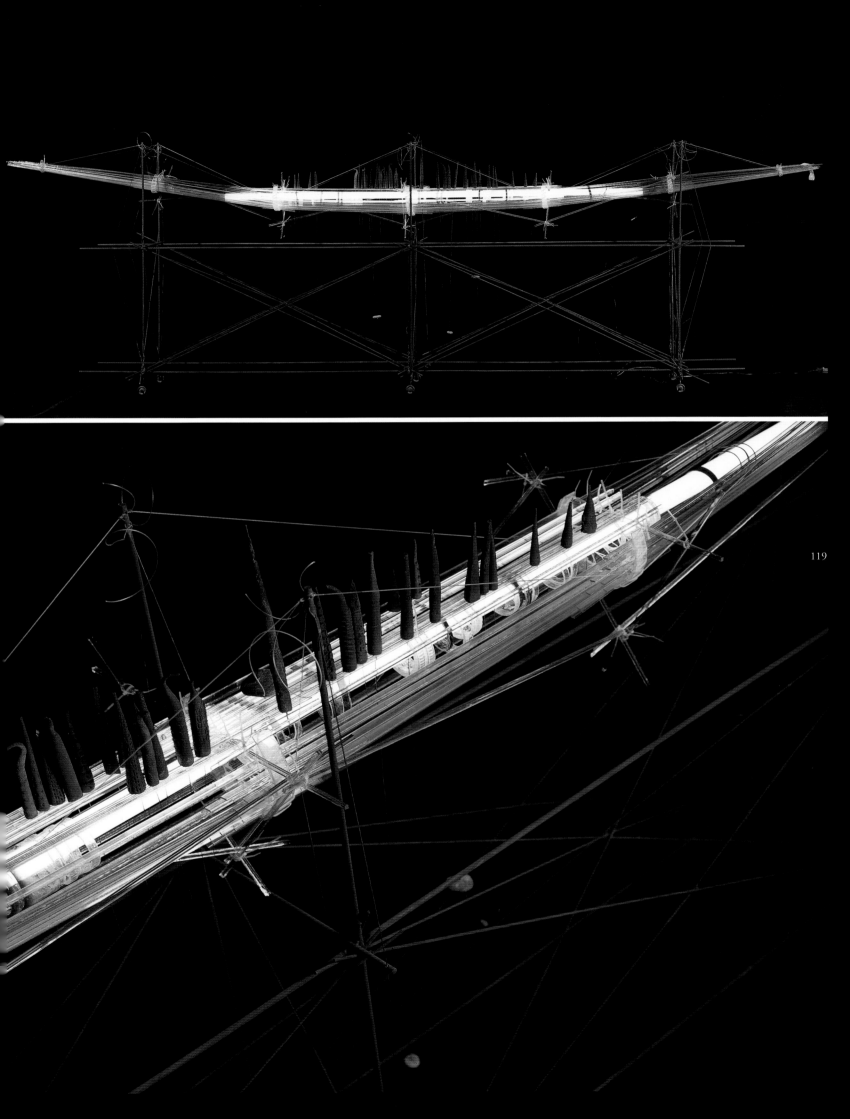

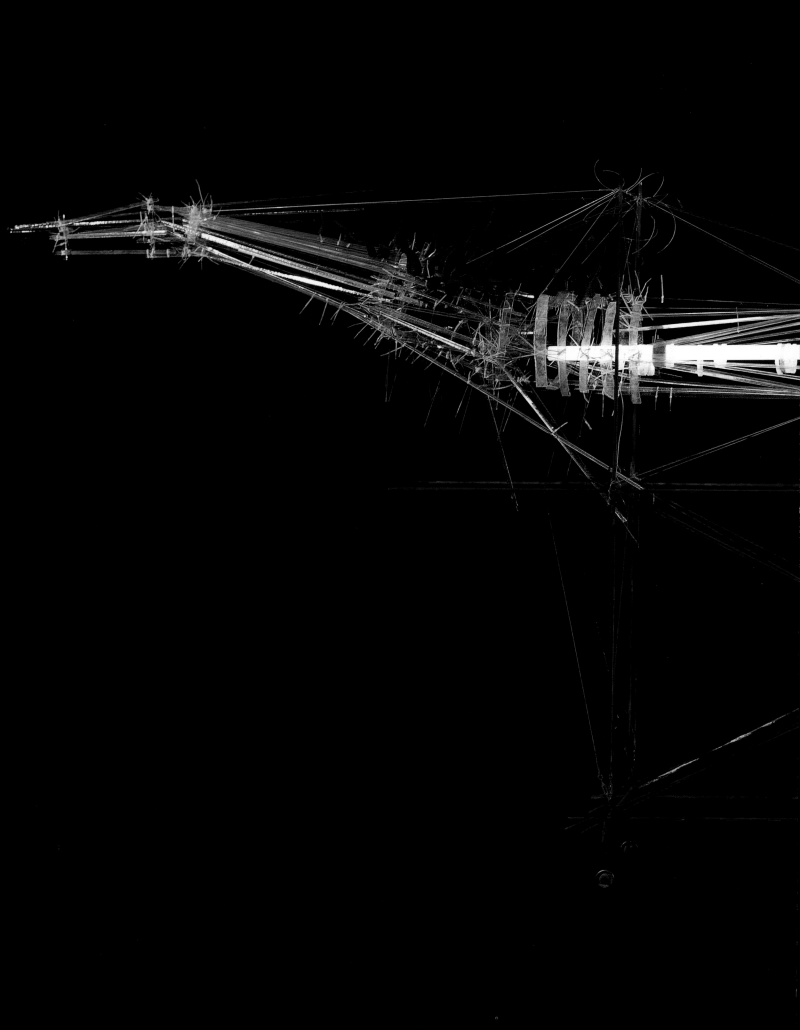

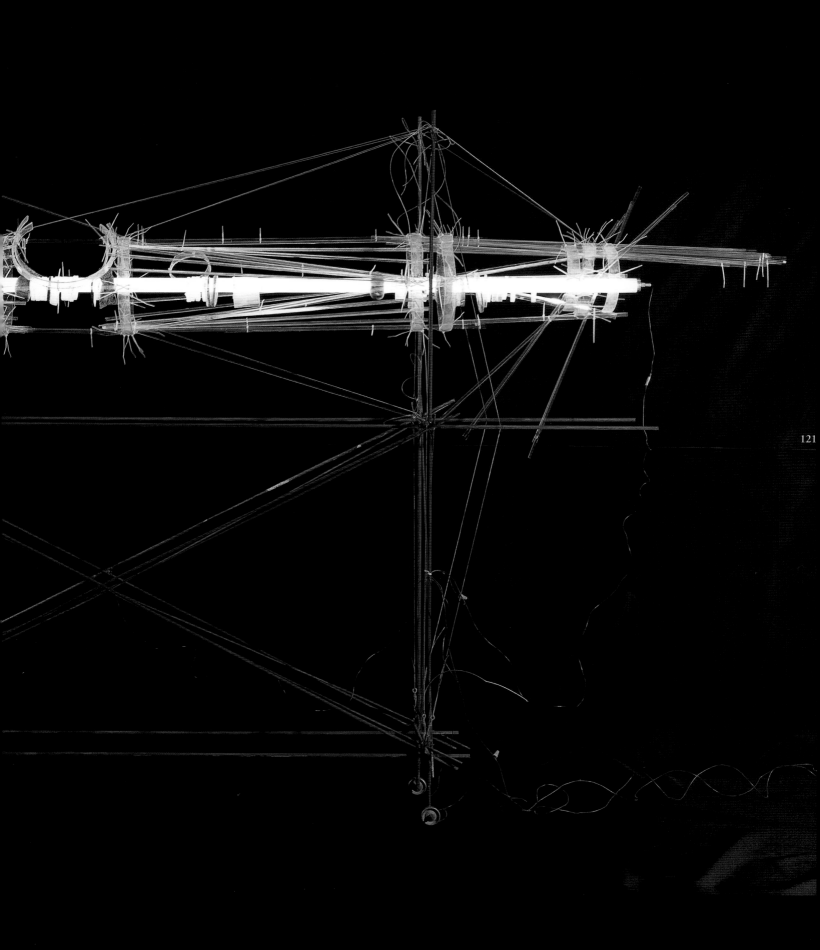

124

Act III
POISONED GARDEN OF EARTHLY DELIGHTS

I often dream of the stage as a garden. Sometimes I imagine a Japanese garden—a place of contemplation, where every stone has consciousness, every stone is a microcosm of the Earth. Sometimes, I see a Piranesi-like space with overgrown ruins, as if all the layers of civilizations are compressed; the entire Earth is encapsulated in that place. It is a place of myth, memory, history, and time.

Time is central in opera. It makes opera design different from any other visual art. You deal with time on two levels: the actual time-music-rhythm of the performance, and time as historical memory.

The ultimate, possibly unattainable, goal as you create an opera is to make the sets come alive and move in time-music-rhythm—to create an event, a transformation, a metamorphosis. These moments are always climactic, heart-stopping moments for the audience. They are the essence of the magic of theater.

One can imagine time as a spiral: the future upward and the past downward. Paradoxically, each new development in art simultaneously moves into the past. Each turn of the spiral opens one more archaic layer. New art strives for more and more ancient archetypes. The Russian avant-garde and futurism were obsessed with the past, with the archaic, with myth. They imagined an epochal split between the West and the East, between the "geometric" sensibility of the West, and the "algebraic" East. It was a search for Mongol, Scythian, Eurasian roots. Eclectics, dissonance, and the quilt of disparate cultures became ways to reach for the harmony of the "music of the spheres."

As the masters of the avant-garde did before me, I imagine the creation of a world museum where the soul remembers the past.

I hear the whisper of destiny as needles of the Norns, the magical fates, are weaving the endless cloth of time. Eternity wipes out traces of time. Man before eternity has no face. The horizon behind man is no longer the Earth—it is dust, patches of color, dematerialized matter. In Malevich's *Victory Over the Sun*, the outside world disappears. Turning itself inside out like a glove, it becomes a curled up dimension of string theory. In one of the ominous images of the twisted, inside-out space, houses have windows looking inside and they seem to be moving. There is no light, no sun, no sky. We find ourselves on the inside surface of the hollow Earth. That space is formed by the ripped-off sun, which used to grow roots deep into the ground. Not only the sun, but also the past, is destroyed. What we are left with is the present. The events of the future are predetermined by the ancient past, as if the future comes before the past. Akin to a mythic serpent biting its own tail, it turns the universe and time inside out. The future feels more like the poisoned garden of earthly delights.

Planet Earth Gallery

The purpose of the Earth Center was to show not only the problems threatening the earth, but also their solutions. Like Hieronymus Bosch's *The Garden of Earthly Delights*, it creates an effect of paradise where something is not right.

The Millennium Commission sponsored the project and found a former mine to contain it. A great deal can be said of ecology, but there is no text here; everything is experienced emotionally. We were inspired by the Japanese haiku, in which nature is described as momentary impressions. We thus created the installation with sensors that react to the movements and behavior of visitors as if reacting to the population of the Earth. When a certain number of people act in a certain way, the room "explodes." For instance, it fills up with a gigantic wave. You sense the beauty and the scale of the ocean, but feel that somehow something is not right, and you understand that the water is poisoned. These megamoments end variously. It is easy to show destruction. New beginnings are much harder (sunlight serves this aim). People react like a flying saucer has landed: they fall into a trance.

There were also huge glass spheres, poured by sculptors in my studio in New York, in the installation. At the entrance is a sphere with the most pessimistic possible development: the Earth has already died. Then there were three spheres demonstrating the three most fearful threats to the ecology—nuclear, chemical, and everyday pollution. At the exit a final sphere contains a prism that refracts sunlight.

In the center is a Stonehenge built of glass plates on which basic concepts like the cosmos, birds, fish, and people were represented by handmade earthen sculptures in the spirit of African art. After passing through them you found yourself at a pool of water with a small, glass, very delicate, blue Earth in the center.

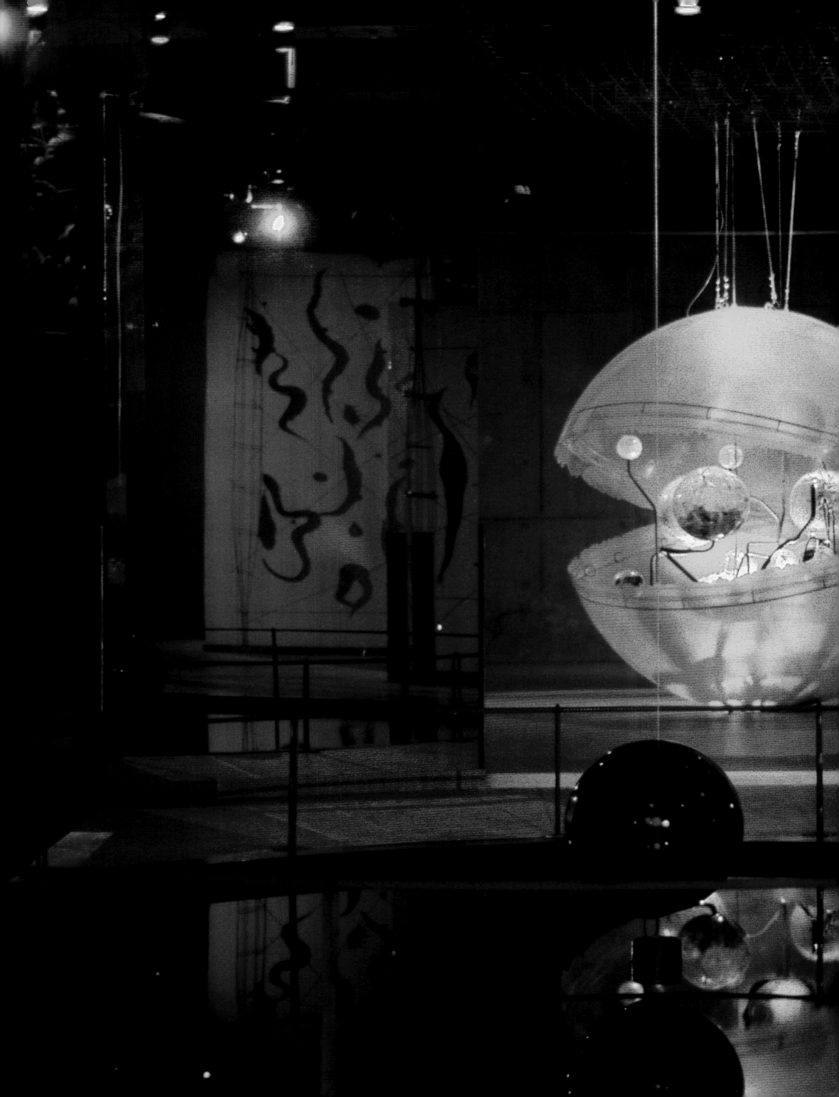

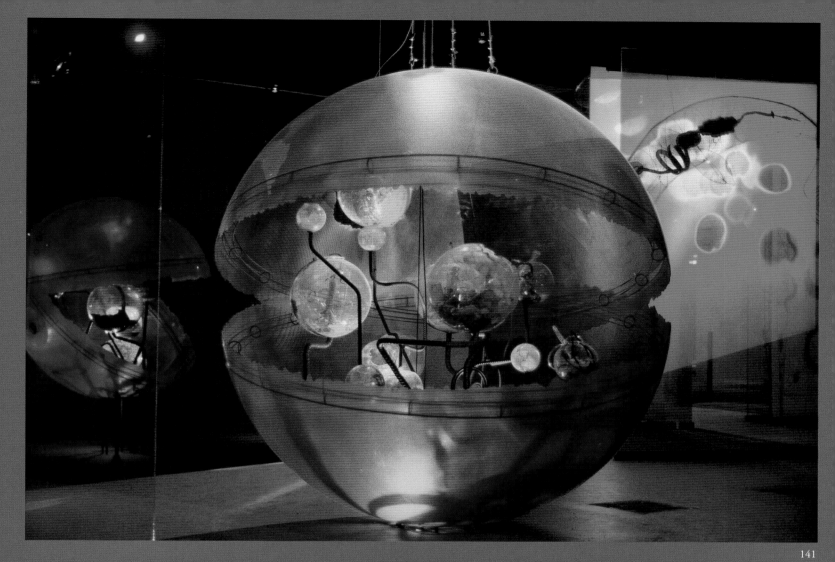

Theodora

Theodora is about the conflict between the Romans and the first Christians. It is George Händel's conversation with God. The subject defies any visual representation unless you take a very personal, subjective route, completely mysterious even to yourself. I discovered a long time ago that the more peculiar, subtle, personal, and seemingly accessible only to myself something is the more people will respond to it.

The set for *Theodora* is the most mysterious I have ever designed: I have no idea what it means. I knew I had stumbled onto something when my heart started beating over an incident that I myself did not understand. I was at the Victoria and Albert Museum, and all of a sudden I saw a display of ancient glass in a glowing fluorescent light box; I knew it was the set for *Theodora*. Back in my studio, we broke glass bottles, glued them back together, and put them in a fluorescent box until we were happy with the results. The only remaining task was to blow this thing up.

The thirty-three-foot bottles were built without any supporting structure. They moved slowly around the stage. Sometimes they looked like a heavenly city, sometimes like mountains, caves, or clouds. They were reminiscent of silhouettes of the saints, but also of the shapes of female bodies. During the production I decided they represented the subtle auras of human shapes. Now I think that they might represent a three-dimensional form of vibrations from the string theory—the stuff of which the universe is made.

Symphony for the Earth

Famous musicians on all continents were hooked up via satellites to a studio set in Tokyo, from which Seiji Ozawa conducted the World Orchestra. The set represented an inverted half globe "floating on flowers" in a black pond. Inside the globe, there were enormous slide projections with images of the Earth (mountains, sky, sea of humanity), and video images of all the participants. A glass bridge connected the globe to another island, which the conductor crossed to lead the live orchestra. I conceived the set in such a way that it could be filmed mainly from cranes. The resulting camera shots created a constant dizzying effect of flying over the set, the performers, the Earth. The four-hour program was seen by more than a billion viewers.

The Grand Macabre

The place is a nuclear reactor somewhere in the Nevada desert. The time is the end of the world. Strange bubbles of deadly energy are about to burst from their concrete containers. The apocalyptic Buddha-like horse with a thousand arms has a thousand legs.

When I build a model, I often have to go through a crisis, a little apocalypse in its own right. I was breaking and exploding old television sets. I was trying to cast huge light bulbs in plaster, and they kept blowing up inside. I was experimenting with toxic materials in order to capture the dangerous "end of the world" atmosphere of the opera. Strangely, all that effort somehow translated into the actual set and gave a shape to the whole production.

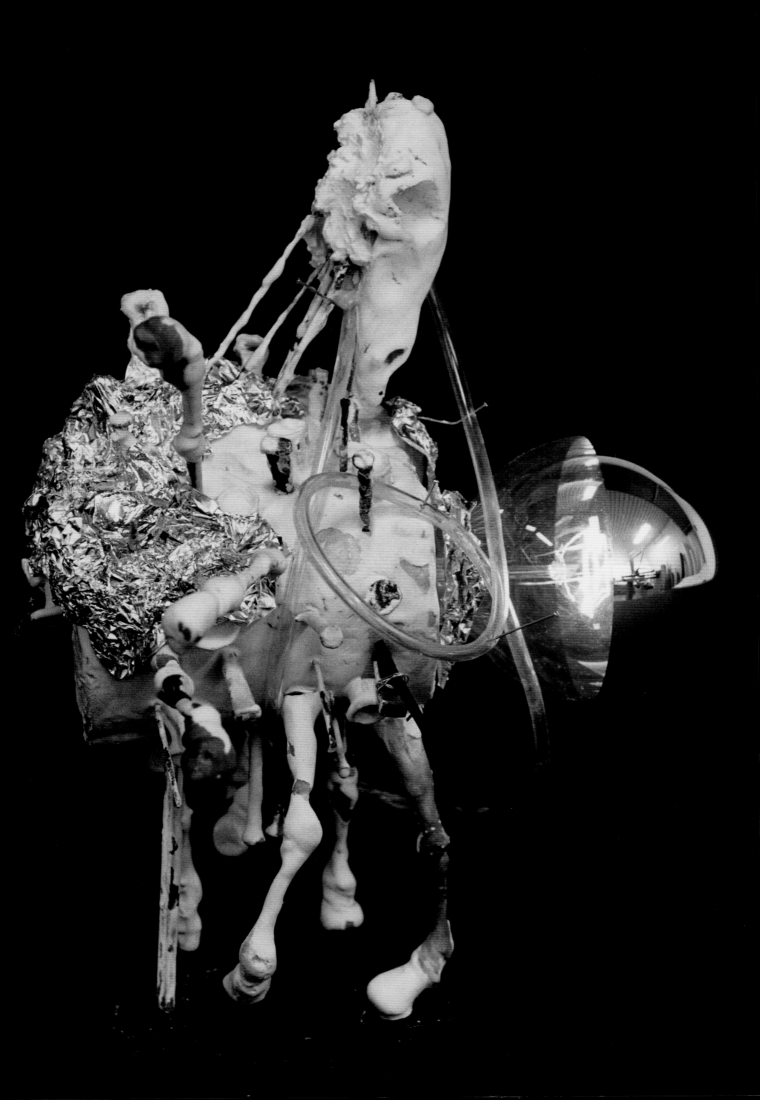

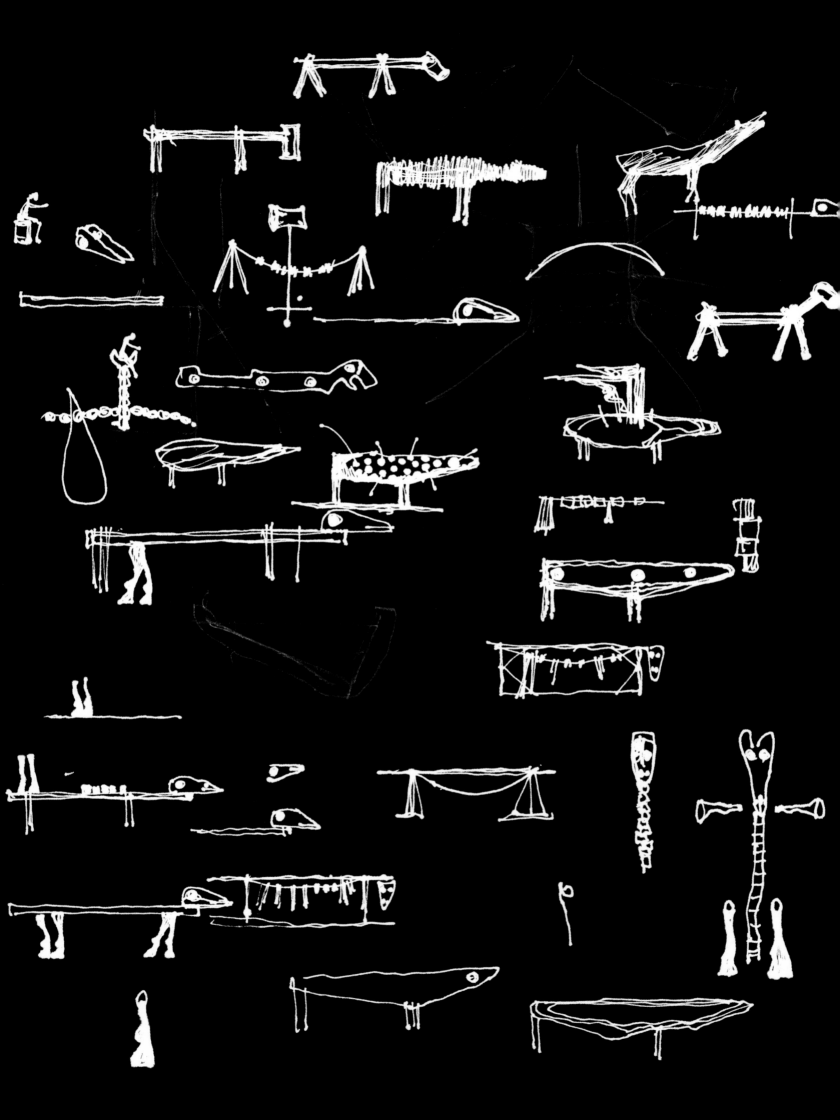

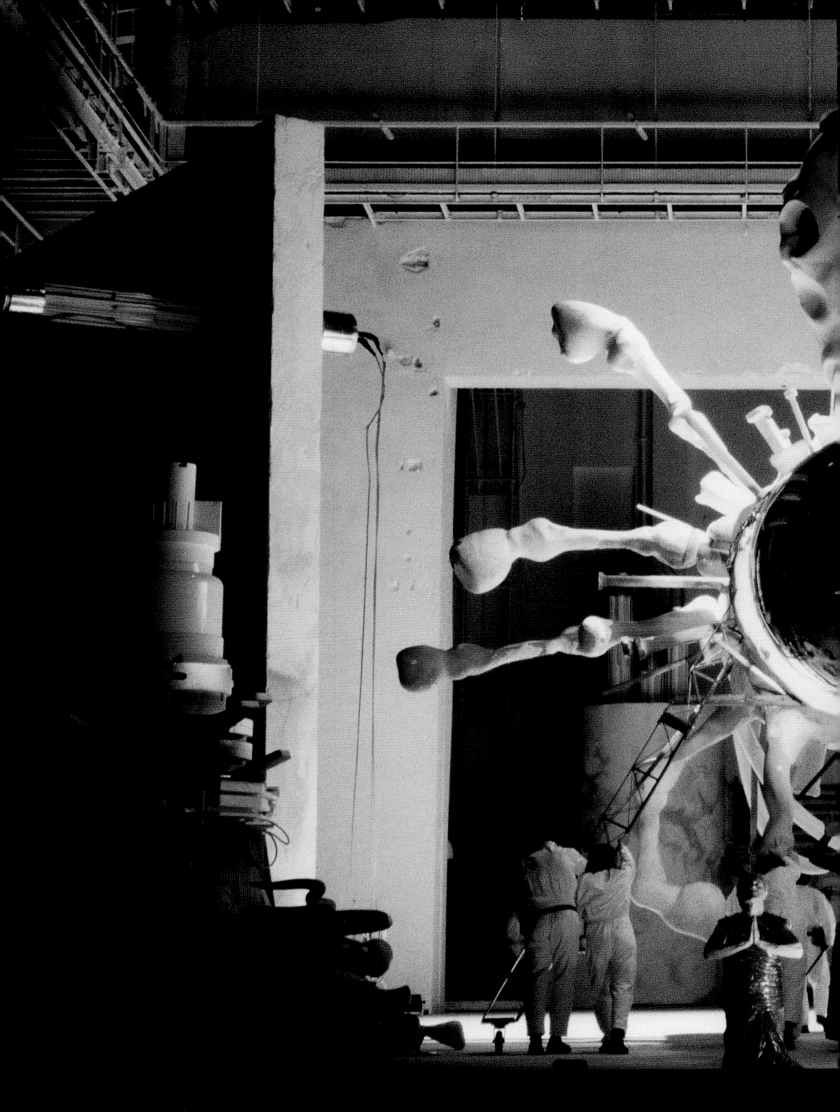

The Ring Cycle (Saint Petersburg)

There is a sense in Richard Wagner's *The Ring Cycle* that nature and people are impure, contaminated by insatiable greed. Today's world of genetically altered food, cloning, and the consequences of tampering with life itself seems to be even more dangerous.

I wanted to create a world onstage where the line between the humans and the artificial creatures is blurred. The stage is dominated by four giant figures morphing into horses, trees, mountains, fire, clouds, and architecture. They become the dragon, they form Valhalla and Gibichung Castle. They represent the four operas of the cycle, the four seasons, the four directions, and the four elements. They are the silent witnesses, cosmic creatures playing their own drama, telling their own meta-story onstage. To be sure, each of their movements, each gesture, each turn of their heads might have taken them a thousand years (twenty minutes in operatic terms), but these were primordial beings with emotions relating to the performers and each other. They came alive from the past.

The figures' presence onstage makes the humans more vulnerable; the giants become the witnesses, protectors, and caretakers. Brunhilde goes into her eternal sleep in the chest cavity of one of the giants as the other three become the circle of fire. One of the giants becomes the mold for making the sword in *Siegfried*. They grow wings and become guardian angels in *Die Walküre,* and they slowly kneel and pray as Siegfried and Brunhilde make love. Sometimes they show emotion as their hearts begin to pulse, sometimes they seem to be thinking as their brains light up. But most of the time they remain indifferent.

The stage is inhabited by some other small mysterious creatures (Nibelungs?) who also seem to escape definition, at times appearing as underwater organisms (*Das Rheingold*), hot coals (*Die Walküre*), tree trunks (*Siegfried*), and triumphant conquerors (*Götterdämmerung*). Our seemingly apolitical approach became strangely subversive. Instead of a quintessential myth about a German national idea, it was a search for universal myth.

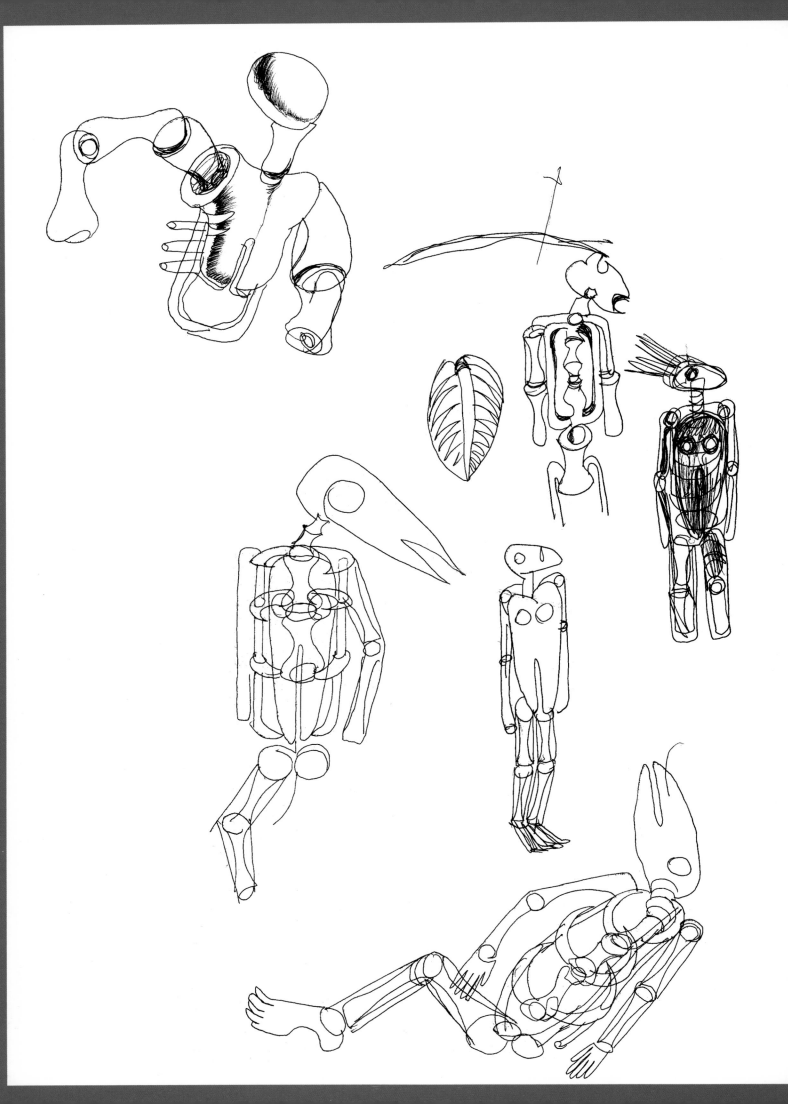

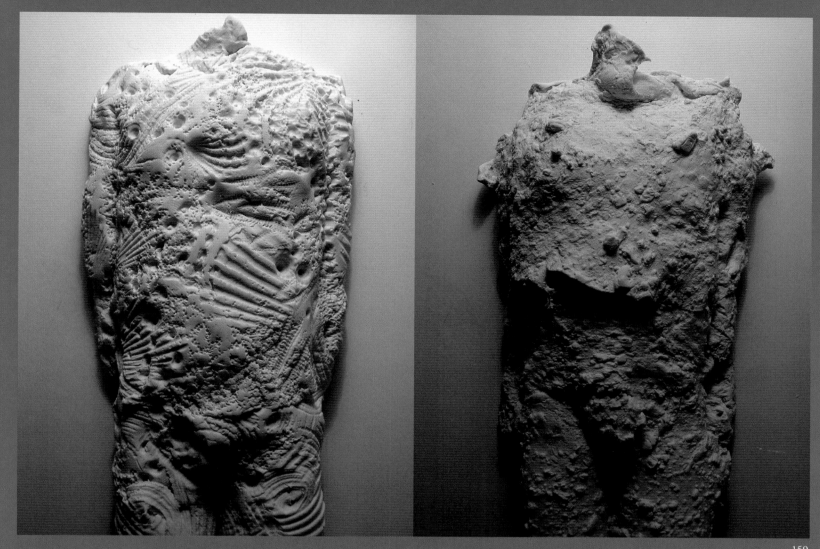

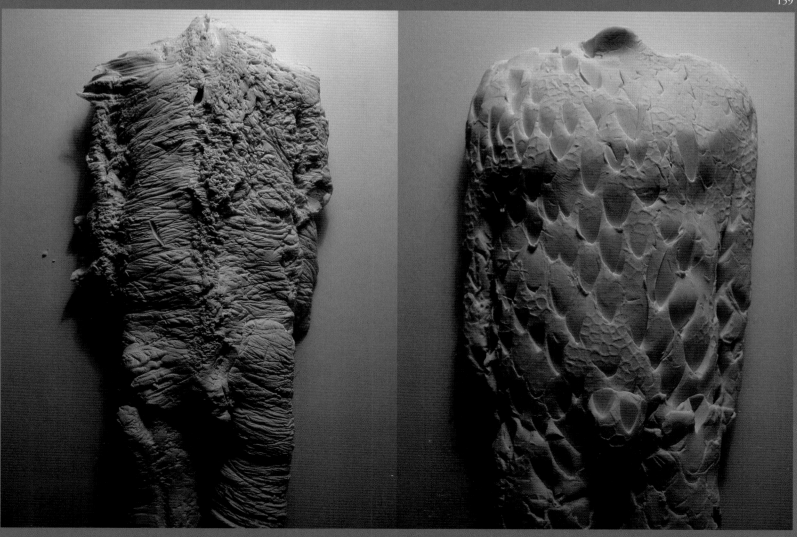

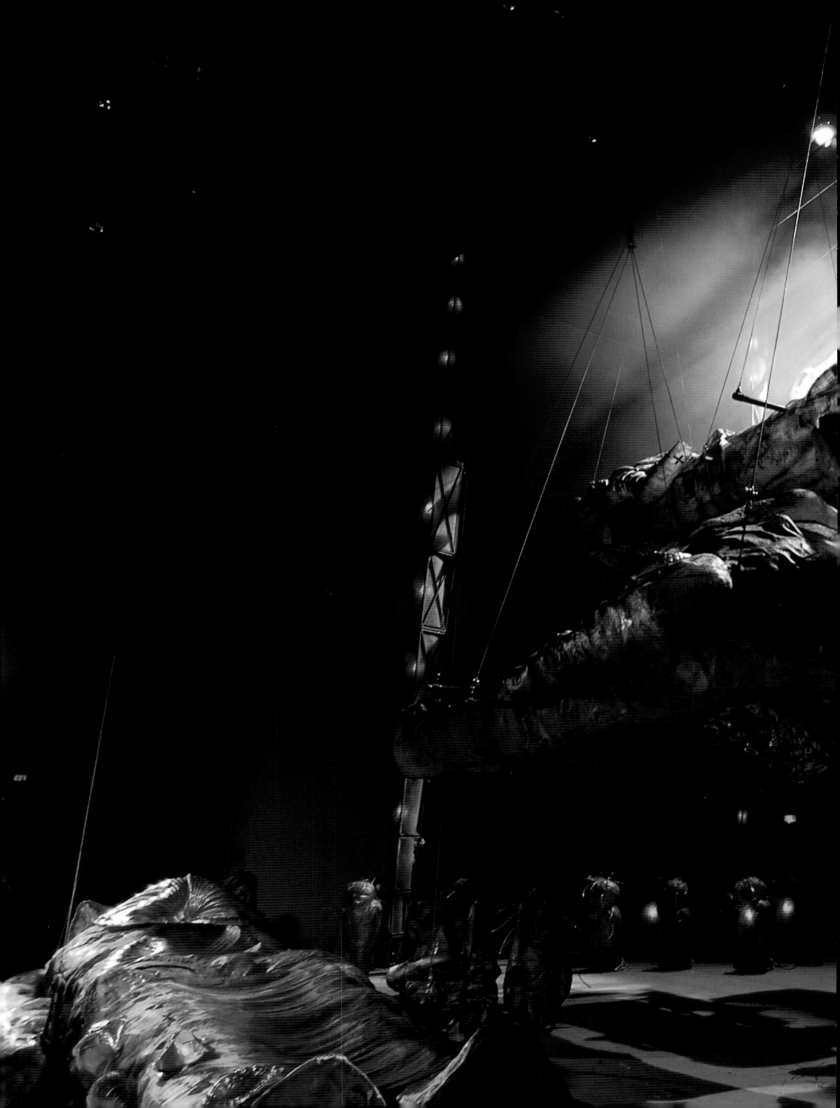

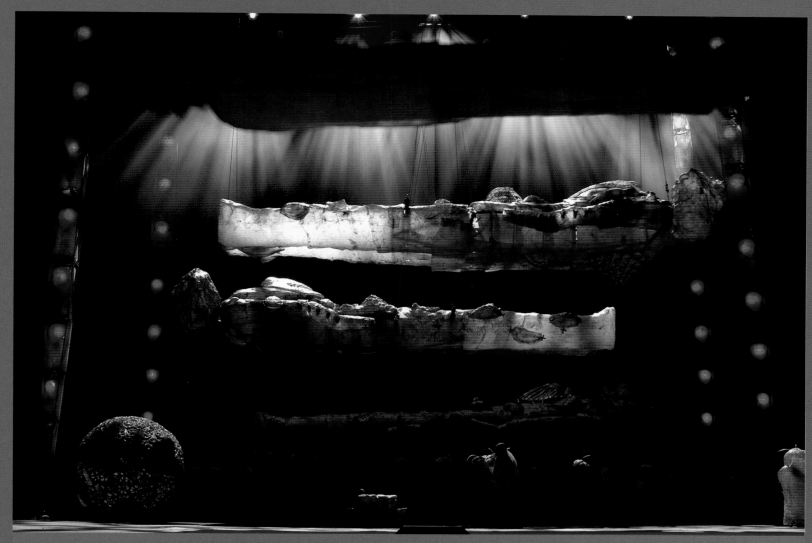

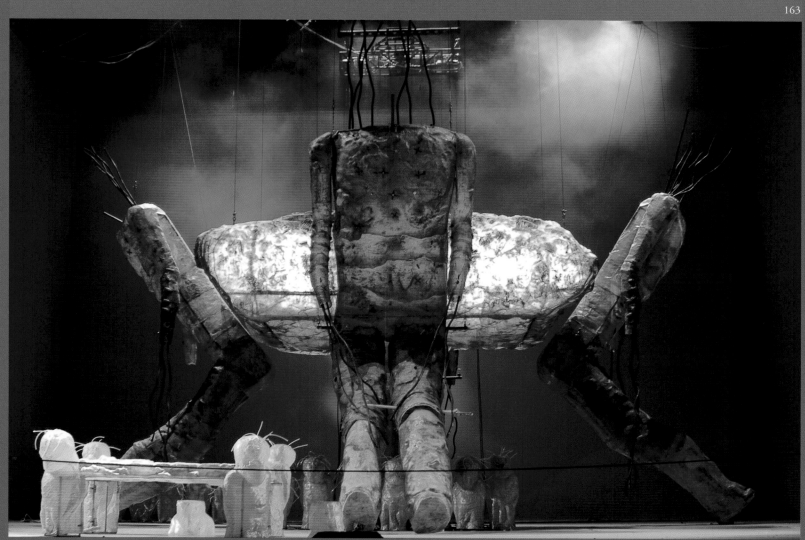

Act IV
FIRE: BURN WITHOUT A TRACE

Metaphorically speaking, the emotional climax of a performance is fire. The final apocalyptic transformation becomes a nightmarish vision of the stage catching fire. The theater itself—the world—is on fire. In the final catharsis there is a fusion of the creative fire, of the composer, director, designer, performers, and the audience. Metaphorically, they are burning together. They are an enormous purifying ball of fire, a white hot sun scorching our souls. And then there is nothing. We burn without a trace.

The whole performance strives toward light. I design for light, making everything of glass, which is materialized light. Light directly corresponds to music. Out of original blackness the light is born. White light is the presence of all color. Operatic performance moves toward this apocalyptic explosion of light, towards final destruction, in order to start from the beginning and create anew.

The central image in opera is the sun, as the ultimate source of light, the mythic fire. The sun also expresses God, vision, eyesight, time, light, sky, movement, death, sundown, and eclipse. The sun represented as an eye is a symbol of the artist's vision, as if having two eyes in the back of the head gives an artist the ability to build in four dimensions, including time. There are biblical images of fantastic animals with eyes in front and back. And blindness itself can create a source of special vision.

In the cosmology of the Russian avant-garde there are three suns: white, red, and black. When primordial Earth is scorched by the three suns, life becomes impossible. Velimir Khlebnikov's mythic hero attacks two suns, red and black, and destroys them with a spear. The three suns in Khlebnikov's universe correspond to three kinds of language: black is protohuman beyond-sense, the noise of creation, and the bird language of archaic gods and demons; red is the language of future superhumans; and white is the normal human language. The parallel to the three worlds of Gods, giants, and Nibelungs is obvious. Kazimir Malevich also has three ways of depicting the sun: the heavenly wheel, black semicircle, and black semicircle with black rays in the shape of flames.

When the sun is destroyed, a huge amount of "emptiness" will be released, creating a euphoria of lightness. It is the euphoria of the absence of logic, the black hole of nonsense discovered on the other side of reason, consciousness, and experience, where time and memory are wiped out as well. Time does not exist without us.

As my work enters into non-objectivity, with no remnants of nature and the real world, what is left? I find myself in a desert where nothing is real, except feeling. It is a terrifying prospect: relying on feelings and intuition. It requires a lot of will and confidence to make hundreds of people work and spend millions of dollars on something I imagined in the middle of the night.

As I make that terrifying leap and let my intuition take over, I create a whole new universe with its own laws, logic, and syntax; I have to allow my consciousness to expand to the size of that whole universe. This also means abandoning all objects, all notions of the material, the permanent, and the physical. I have to confront emptiness as Malevich did when he created empty canvases at the end of his life.

Why is it that theater—this most ephemeral, seemingly inconsequential form of art—becomes an obsession dominating my whole being? It requires total commitment: I have to burn without a trace. Once the show is over, there is nothing left. The audience is gone; I will never know what they felt, or whether they felt anything. The sets are usually destroyed. The show cannot really be recorded; the photographs are totally inadequate.

It took me a long time to realize that I should not hold on to these unique moments, because their ephemeral quality is exactly what makes them so powerful. The intensity of each experience comes from an almost physical pain of losing each moment. Each moment is unique, never to be duplicated. Its evanescent, fleeting nature resonates with our sense of mortality and makes it that much more poignant. The piercing beauty of every second of this life makes me understand how jealous the gods must be of us, the mortals.

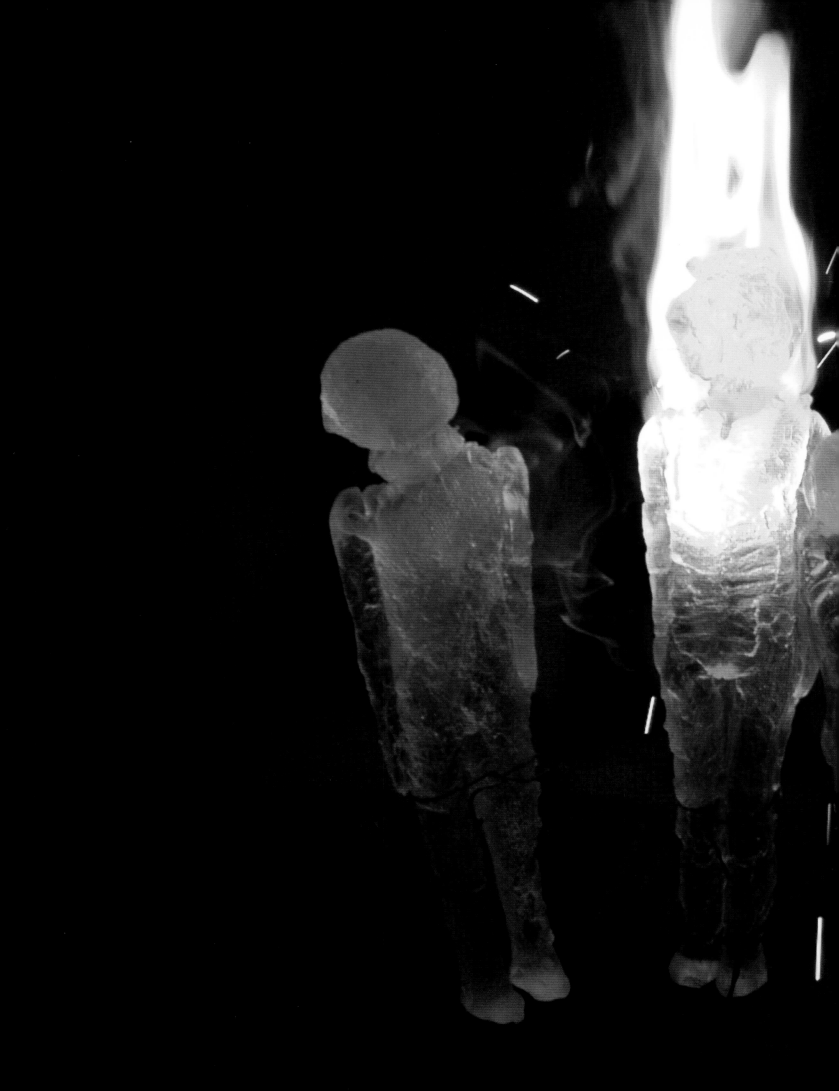

The Magic Flute

The Magic Flute is a Masonic opera; the plot is complicated and ultimately nonsensical. It can only be understood as a spiritual journey. The design for it is a crystal temple. As you enter this temple, you enter your inner world, made of glass and mirrors. It is full of mysterious symbols: Tantric, Egyptian, Oriental, Chinese. It is the world of alchemy and crystal balls, the world of transparent ephemeral architecture. You go through round, square, and triangular vaults. The temple architecture breaks into fragments and then reassembles itself, always in a new unpredictable way. Spaces form in front of your eyes and dissolve. It is an architecture in constant flux. It is a labyrinth, and we as an audience are taken through it.

You find yourself inside an enormous kaleidoscope, the world is shattered into fractals, reflections upon reflections, taking you into endless space. The mirror becomes a main metaphor, a vessel of your soul. There is a magic separation between the light and darkness, the male energy of the sun (Zarastro) and the female energy of darkness (Queen of the Night). This separation becomes a window, a door: once you go through it, you change your nature.

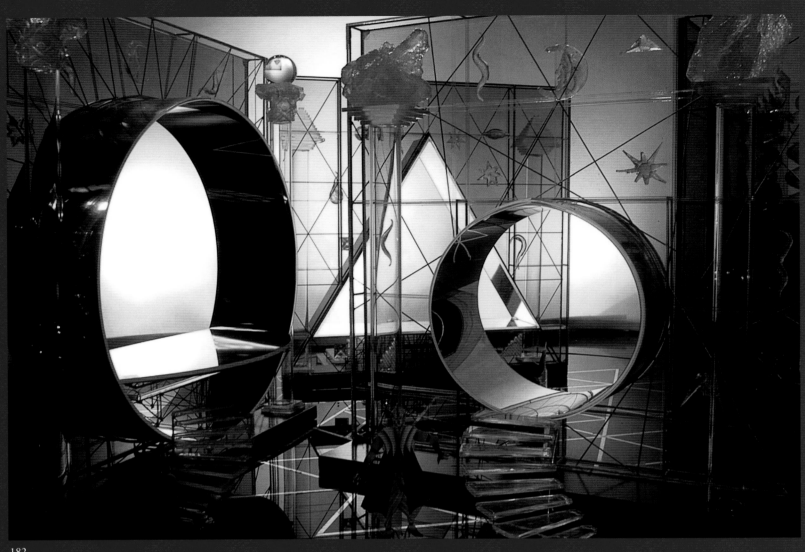

182

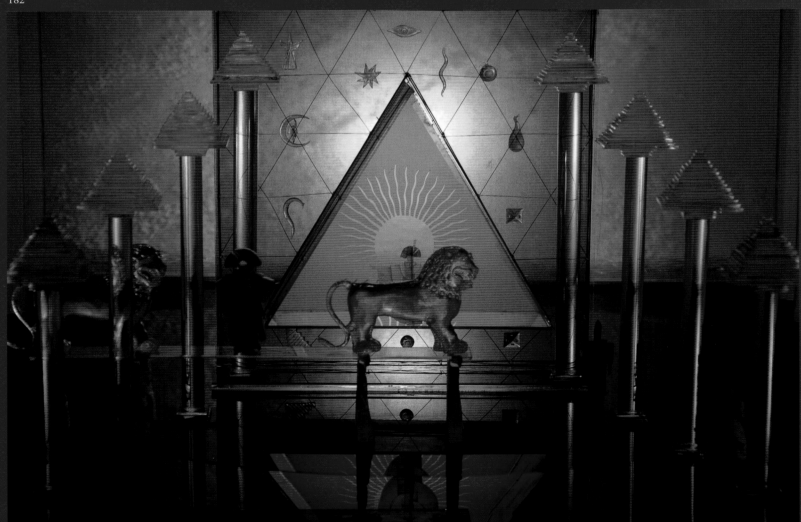

Les Troyens

On the site that once was Troy, there are at least nine layers of civilizations. There is a war of civilizations taking place right now, and there will be others in the future. *Les Troyens* is an opera about civilizations rising and collapsing, new ones emerging and disappearing again. Enormous stone columns, vaguely resembling the Twin Towers, are being erected and collapsing throughout the course of the opera. The whole set rose from a lake in a subterranean cave, with dancing glass trees above and a realistic satyr built by an animatronics specialist from Hollywood. The four forty-five-foot legs of the horse appear first, then we see the head of the horse taking up the whole stage.

I wanted to create a dizzying effect for the audience, one of falling and rising through endless levels of an imaginary space, through layers of different cultures, and through time. In the final scene, a glass Trojan boat—the symbol of hope and the future, which we see throughout the whole evening—takes off from the ground as a cosmic object and turns into the Coliseum in front of our eyes.

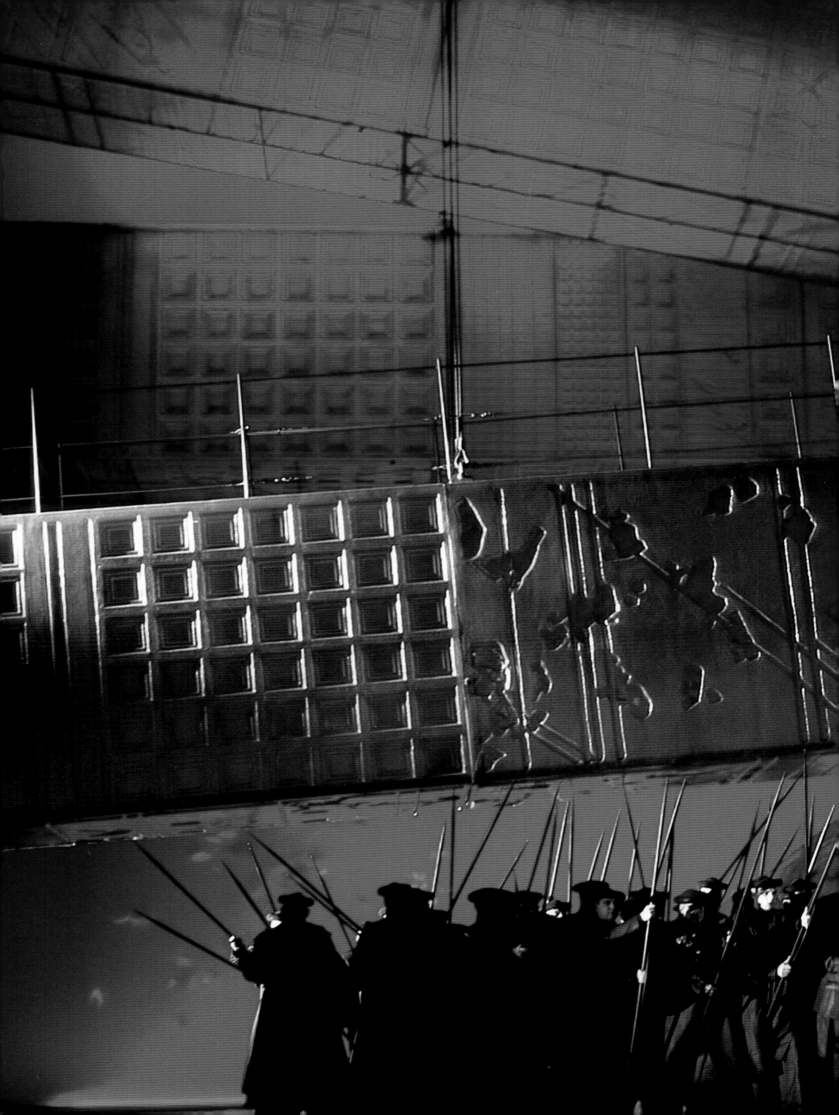

Don Giovanni

Don Giovanni is set in Spanish Harlem amid drugs, crime, and prostitution. You see a realistic section of the street with an abandoned church, an empty parking lot with graffiti and barbed wire, La Famosa Grocery Store, a laundromat, a construction site with a flashing emergency light, and the exposed earth. Don Giovanni is the head of the street gang, and all the other characters live in this place. The reality of the place is reinforced with every detail; nothing really changes on stage during the performance. That is, until the end. The last ten minutes are perhaps the most powerful music Mozart wrote, and all hell breaks loose on stage to accompany it. This very real, recognizable place turns into an enormous Apocalyptic vision as the building slowly moves to the right, the earth begins to open, and the facades crack. As the set opens like an altar piece, hellish creatures inspired by Giotto appear in the windows, the coffin starts flying upward, the emergency streetlight and a fluorescent cross on the church flash wildly, and finally the entire chorus, naked, appears out of the earth as the rising dead—the world ends.

Fiery Angel

This opera's libretto is based on a symbolist novel by Valery Brusov, while its music was written later and has an avant-garde edginess and drive. I was interested in the tension between symbolism and avant-garde and wanted to create a set that had a symbolist atmosphere: a Saint Petersburg courtyard, a well with decaying walls, broken gutters, doors leading nowhere, useless wires, ghosts, and spirits.

The set is a communal apartment where everyone knows everyone else. The madness and visions of Renata, the main character, are the only possible reactions to this type of place. The only way out is death. In her final apocalyptic vision the walls and sections of the floor with sinks and bathtubs swing open like some constructivist wings of an angel. The space explodes, turning into an aggressive deconstructivist nightmare full of jagged lines, a flaming sky, and a bloody floor.

In this three-dimensional labyrinth, neighbors appear as transparent angels, shadows of the young, old, pregnant, and long dead. An enormous elevator shaft tilts forward, seemingly collapsing on the audience. In its blinding column of light, Renata ascends into the sky.

202

War and Peace

When I worked on Prokofiev's opera, *War and Peace*, I decided to put the entire action on the earth and in the sky. Supposedly when Leo Tolstoy wrote the title, he really meant *War and the World*. Whether this is true or not, there is no question that he was dealing with the world in his novel.

I had been obsessing about the globe shape for a while. It suggested the form of a Russian onion dome and a pregnant woman's body. So the whole first act takes place on a strangely convex parquet floor. It gives all the interior scenes an eerie, surrealistic look, yet it also gives a very contemporary cinematic perception of a fish-eye lens, so somehow you are getting a close-up and long shot at the same time.

In the second act, the earth is crushed and breaks open, revealing corpses and mutilated bodies to show remnants of endless wars and suffering. The sky, by contrast, is magical, esoteric, dreamlike, ephemeral, and constantly changing. It is the famous tall sky that the dying Andrei Bolkonski sees when he is fatally wounded. People's actions, destinies, and lives seem small and inconsequential next to this sky. As for the vision of the sacred burning city of Moscow behind the sky, people could not believe the audacity of putting most of the set—that is, the expense—behind a plastic drop so that all the audience could see was a faint mirage of the city. It is Moscow, which every Russian was willing to burn so that Napoleon could not conquer it. It is a Moscow that is no longer there, a lost spiritual dimension.

Encore

I Never Know Where We Will Be Going

Julie Taymor

George and I met in the early nineties at his studio to look at his portfolio and to discuss our future collaboration. I was immediately struck by the daring uniqueness of his work. George is an architect and a sculptor, which is essential to his stage designs. I was thrilled with his whimsical play with perspective and with the dangerous aspects of scenic elements. A two-lane highway jutted out from a back wall twenty feet up in the air, precarious and aggressive. Canals of Venice turned on their sides in extreme forced perspective. Nothing about George's work was mundane, safe, or set. In fact, he was not a set designer but more of an architect of environment.

I wanted a designer to challenge me, to bring me to places that my own imagination would not necessarily bring me. I wanted a visual poet who could get to the essence of a piece in a nonliteral manner. The way that we worked on *Oedipus* and then on four subsequent opera productions was to explore the core ideas of the libretto searching for an ideograph of the whole. In the case of *Oedipus* it was the eye. George's design idea was a stage that was flooded with water above which floated an enormous stylized eye made of slatted bent wood. The eyelids were a platform and a suspended ceiling whose textures and materials fit in with a Japanese aesthetic. We worked together on many details that also included puppet elements and physical, visual, moving stage actions. Nothing seemed impossible with George. And some scenic elements completely surprised us with their effect once graced with lighting. That is always a pleasure even when it could be a disaster. The rear metallic screen cyclorama proved to be a phenomenal transformative event. It looked like stone in one scene, like pure gold in another, and finally it worked much like a traditional scrim.

How light plays off of the materials of a set figures prominently in George's design process. In the production of *The Magic Flute* for the Metropolitan Opera, George created glass geometric kaleidoscopes that are illuminated from within and without. The result is a *Magic Flute* that is illusionary and playful—a true magic box of wonders. His work is not about place as much as it is about feel, mood, and the power of transformation. It is pure theater in that it relies on the participation of the audience to fill in the blanks.

George Tsypin is one of the greatest designers working today at challenging the very art form of live theater. His vision is big and bold and can only be appreciated in the three dimensions of space. I look forward to our next collaboration because I never know in advance where we will be going.

215

010642607

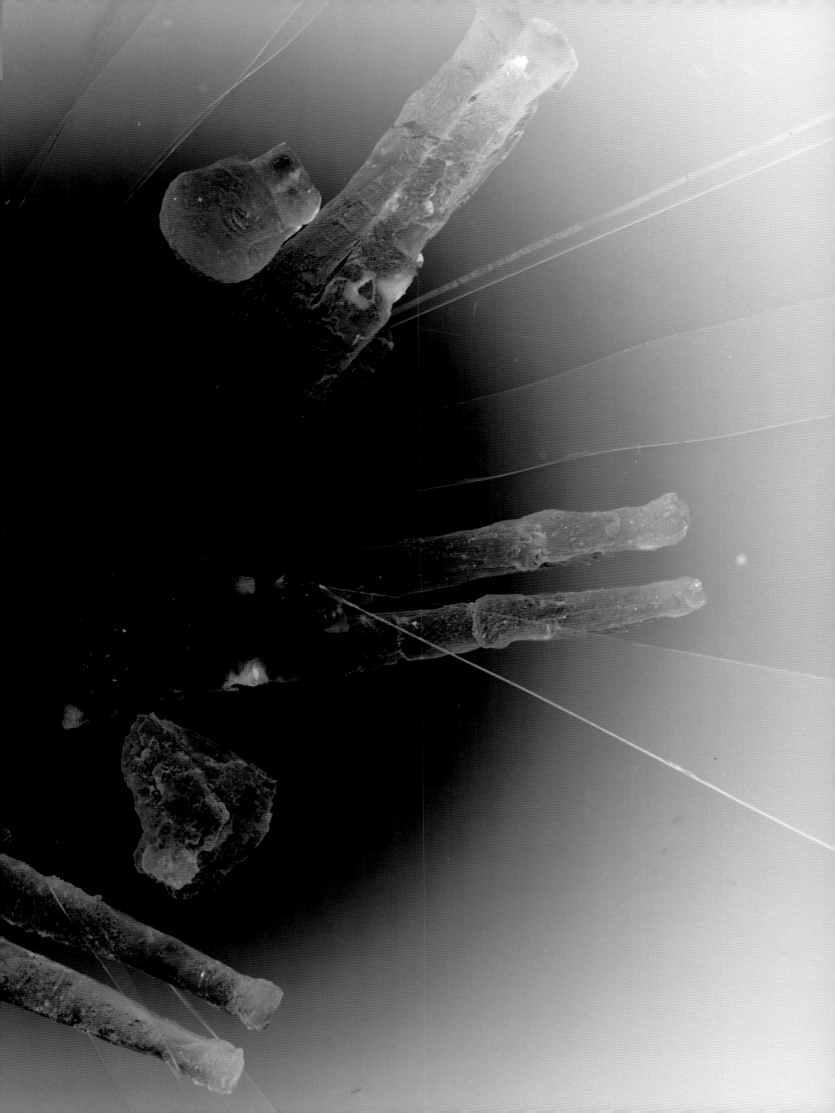

218

Credits

Death in Venice
composed by Benjamin Britten
1984
Conceptual set model: George Tsypin

Oedipus Rex
text by Jean Cocteau
composed by Igor Stravinsky
Saito Kinen Festival, Matsumoto,
    Japan, 1992
Director: Julie Taymor
Sets: George Tsypin
Costumes: Emi Wada
Lights: Jean Kalman

Boris Godunov
composed by Modest Mussorgsky
Mariinsky Theater, St. Petersburg, Russia;
    La Scala, Milan, Italy, 2002
Director: Victor Kramer
Sets: George Tsypin
Costumes: Tatiana Noginova
Lights: Gleb Filshtinsky

Russian Pavilion
Venice Biennale, Venice, Italy, 2002
Overall design: George Tsypin Opera Factory and
    Eugene Monakhov
Artist: Josef Yusupov
Sculptor: Arturo Virtmanis
Music: Bruce Odland

L'Amour de Loin
composed by Kaija Saariaho
Salzburg Festival, Salzburg, Austria, 2001
Director: Peter Sellars
Sets: George Tsypin
Costumes: Martin Pakledinaz
Lights: James Ingalls

Pelléas et Mélisande
composed by Claude Debussy
Netherlands Opera, Amsterdam, The Netherlands,
    1993; Los Angeles Opera, Los Angeles, 1993
Director: Peter Sellars
Sets: George Tsypin
Costumes: Dunya Ramicova
Lights: James Ingalls

West Side Story
composed by Leonard Bernstein
Bregenz Festival, Bregenz, Austria, 2003–04
Director: Francesca Zambello
Sets: George Tsypin
Costumes: Marie-Jeanne Lecca
Lights: James Ingalls

Saint Francis of Assisi
composed by Olivier Messiaen
Salzburg Festival, Salzburg, Austria, 1992;
    Bastille Opera, Paris, France, 1992
Director: Peter Sellars
Sets: George Tsypin
Costumes: Dunya Ramicova
Lights: James Ingalls

Biblical Pieces
composed by Igor Stravinsky
Netherlands Opera, Amsterdam,
    The Netherlands, 1999
Director: Peter Sellars
Sets: George Tsypin
Costumes: Gabriel Berry
Lights: James Ingalls

MTV Video Music Awards
Metropolitan Opera, New York, New York, 1999
Production design: George Tsypin

Millennium Cities
The Earth Center, Doncaster, England, 1999
    (unrealized)
Overall visual design: George Tsypin

The Ring Cycle
composed by Richard Wagner
Netherlands Opera, Amsterdam,
    The Netherlands, 1997–99
Director: Pierre Audi
Sets: George Tsypin
Costumes: Eiko Ishioka
Lights: Wolfgang Göbbel

Planet Earth Gallery
The Earth Center, Doncaster, England, 1999
Concept: Bruce Odland and George Tsypin
Music: Bruce Odland and Sam Auinger
Overall visual design: George Tsypin

Theodora
composed by George Händel
Glyndebourne Festival, Glyndebourne,
    England, 1996
Director: Peter Sellars
Sets: George Tsypin
Costumes: Dunya Ramicova
Lights: James Ingalls

Symphony for the Earth
NHK Television, Tokyo, Japan, 1995
Production design: George Tsypin

The Grand Macabre
composed by Gyorgy Ligeti
Salzburg Festival, Salzburg, Austria, 1997
Director: Peter Sellars
Sets: George Tsypin
Costumes: Dunya Ramicova
Lights: James Ingalls

The Ring Cycle
composed by Richard Wagner
Mariinsky Theater, St. Petersburg, Russia, 2003
Production concept: Valery Gergiev and
    George Tsypin
Conductor: Valery Gergiev
Production design: George Tsypin
Costumes: Tatiana Noginova
Lights: Gleb Filshtinksy

The Magic Flute
composed by Wolfgang Amadeus Mozart
Metropolitan Opera, New York, New York, 2004
Director: Julie Taymor
Sets: George Tsypin
Costumes: Julie Taymor
Lights: Don Holder

Les Troyens
composed by Hector Berlioz
Metropolitan Opera, New York, New York, 2002,
   (unrealized); Netherlands Opera, Amsterdam,
   The Netherlands, 2004
Director: Pierre Audi
Sets: George Tsypin
Costumes: Andrea Schmidt-Futterer
Lights: Peter van Praet

Don Giovanni
composed by Wolfgang Amadeus Mozart
PepsiCo Summerfair, Purchase, New York, 1987
Director: Peter Sellars
Sets: George Tsypin
Costumes: Dunya Ramicova
Lights: James Ingalls

Fiery Angel
composed by Sergey Prokofiev
Bolshoi Theater, Moscow, Russia, 2004
Director: Francesca Zambello
Sets: George Tsypin
Costumes: Tatiana Noginova
Lights: Rick Fisher

War and Peace
composed by Sergey Prokofiev
Mariinsky Theater, Saint Petersburg, Russia, 2000;
   Covent Garden, London, England, 2000;
   La Scala, Milan, Italy, 2000 ; Teatro Real,
   Madrid, Spain, 2001; Metropolitan Opera,
   New York, New York,2002
Director: Andrei Konchalovsky
Sets: George Tsypin
Costumes: Tatiana Noginova
Lights: James Ingalls

221

GEORGE TSYPIN OPERA FACTORY

George Tsypin

George Tsypin is a sculptor, architect, and designer of opera. Since he won an International Competition of "New and Spontaneous Ideas for the Theater for Future Generations," his opera designs have been seen all over the world, including the Salzburg Festival, Opera de Bastille in Paris, Covent Garden in London, La Scala in Milan, and the Metropolitan Opera in New York. Tsypin has worked in all major theaters in America; in the 1990s, he expanded his work to include design for film, television, and concerts as well as exhibitions and installations. The first solo gallery show of his sculpture took place in 1991 at the Twining Gallery in New York. He created the Planet Earth Gallery, one of the Millennium Projects in England: a major installation of moving architectural elements, videos, and two

hundred sculptures. Tsypin exhibited his work at the Venice Biennale in 2002. He studied architecture in Moscow and theater design in New York and has won numerous awards. He has worked for many years with renowned directors such as Peter Sellars, Julie Taymor, Pierre Audi, Francesca Zambello, Jürgen Flimm, and Andrei Konchalovsky. He has a special creative relationship with the conductor Valery Gergiev.

Eugene Monakhov

George and Eugene started working together when they were students at the Moscow School of Architecture. Together they became the winners of the competition of "New and Spontaneous Ideas for the Theater for Future Generations." Eugene participated in numerous competitions and won a number of awards. He brought the precision and clarity of an architect to most projects presented in this book. His skills

222

are unrivaled and he has what are called "golden hands." As the head of Eugene Monakhov Studio, he currently practices in Moscow as an architect and interior designer.

Iosef Yusupov

Iosef Yusupov is a painter, set designer, and scenic artist. In his landscape paintings one can see the bright colors of his native Samarkand. After graduating from the Saint Petersburg Institute of Theater, Music, and Cinematography, he designed sets all over Russia and Eastern Europe. His first major success came with the production of *Oedipus Rex* at the Tadzhik Lakhuti Academic Drama Theater, for which he received the prestigious State Prize of the USSR for the Arts. Since moving to the United States, he has designed numerous shows in New York, including plays, operas, and TV, and has worked as a scenic artist on major Hollywood

motion pictures. He has been involved in all George Tsypin Opera Factory productions since the early 1990s as a generator of ideas. Most of the shows of this period would never have happened without his ideas, inspiration, and energy.

Arturs Virtmanis

Arturs Virtmanis is an artist and a sculptor, and was born in Riga, Latvia. He studied at the Latvian Academy of Art, and now lives and works in the U.S. He has been involved in numerous solo and collaborative art projects in the U.S. and in Europe. His work—large-scale drawings, sculptures, and installations—fuses together esoteric and popular aspects of culture and is aimed at revealing a mystical and a transcendental side of the world through seemingly ordinary things or processes.

Published by
Princeton Architectural Press
37 East Seventh Street
New York, New York 10003

For a free catalog of books, call 1.800.722.6657.
Visit our web site at www.papress.com.

All art is by George Tsypin except the following:
Arturs Virtmanis: 41B, 116–117, 135–137, 159
Natasha Rasina: 42–47, 162, 166–170, 172–173
Igor Vishniakov: 49, 115, 119–121
Ruth Walz: 53, 54T, 55, 77, 82–83, 85, 88–89, 98B, 103,
    106T, 110–111, 151, 168–169
Steve Moles: 138–141

Editing: Clare Jacobson
Editorial assistance: Lauren Nelson and Dorothy Ball
Design: Jan Haux

Special thanks to: Nettie Aljian, Nicola Bednarek, Janet
Behning, Penny (Yuen Pik) Chu, Russell Fernandez,
John King, Mark Lamster, Nancy Eklund Later, Linda Lee,
Katharine Myers, Jane Sheinman, Scott Tennent, Jennifer
Thompson, Paul G. Wagner, Joe Weston, and Deb Wood of
Princeton Architectural Press —Kevin C. Lippert, publisher

Library of Congress Cataloging-in-Publication Data
Tsypin, George, 1954-
George Tsypin opera factory : building in the black void /
George Tsypin ; with texts by Julie Taymor and Grigory Revzin.
    p. cm.
  ISBN 1-56898-532-0 (alk. paper)
1. Tsypin, George, 1954- 2. Set designers—Biography.
3. Opera—Stage-setting and scenery. 4. Opera—Production
and direction. I. Taymor, Julie, 1952- II. Revzin, G. I.
(Grigorïi I.) III. Title.
  ML423.T78A3 2005
  792.5'025'092—dc22
                                        2005005836